PRAISE FOR *TRANSVE*

"Urayoán understands the importance of his poetry being accessible. He understands that art is for everyone and so he communicates with everyone. For him, all the dimensions of words are indispensable and therefore phonetics become visible in his stanzas. He respects words not in a professorial way but rather in the same way one respects the standing of an old-school *bichote* who's still alive. Language is not a barrier but an imaginary border that serves as a tool to fatten up the arguments of his words. In life one has to move, one has to walk even when there's a more comfortable way to get somewhere else, to other paths, and if I were to cross over one day, I would do so with this book. The transversal is as necessary as growth."

"Urayoán entiende la importancia de que sus versos sean accesibles. Entiende que el arte es para todos, por eso se comunica con todos. Para él todas las dimensiones de las palabras son imprescindibles, por eso la fonética en sus estrofas se hace visible. Respeta las palabras pero no desde un lugar catedrático sino desde el mismo lugar en el que se respetan los rangos de un bichote vieja escuela que sigue con vida. El idioma no es una barrera sino una frontera imaginaria que sirve como herramienta para engordar los argumentos de sus palabras. En la vida hay que moverse, hay que caminar aunque estemos cómodos para llegar a otros lados, a otros rumbos y si algún día fuese a cruzar, cruzaría con este libro. Lo transversal es tan necesario como crecer."

—RESIDENTE, recording artist and filmmaker

"*Transversal* is what would happen if Mallarmé and Sarduy met cruising on Crane's Brooklyn Bridge; if Pietri and Delany had gone to the march and talked shit about every colonizer; if poems as constellations met poems as remakes and disidentifications were also counteridentifications; and if every classroom were in itself three places: a stage, a cipher, and a living room. I read this book many times. The first was moving between languages. The second, in English. *La tercera, en español.* The fourth, somewhere scattered. Never in that order. In fact, in fact, if language could do everything I ever wanted it to do and then some, it would be this here book. I mean. This. Read it, if you can, and if you can't, read it too."

—RAQUEL SALAS RIVERA, author of *x/ex/exis*, 2018 Ambroggio Prize

"Urayoán Noel is one of the most innovative poets writing today. This book transgresses the lines of translation and transcreation, while also transversing the coordinates of the translingual and the transhemispheric. Throughout, Noel interweaves languages (English, Spanish, and Spanglish) and poetic forms (both traditional and improvisational) to express an archipelagic relationality, a stateless sovereignty, and a queer Boricua imaginary. Ultimately, he shows us how the 'transversal is the light that binds us **transversal es la luz que nos une**.'"

—CRAIG SANTOS PEREZ, author of *Habitat Threshold*

"These masterful poems advance along tracks that sometimes run parallel, sometimes overlap, sometimes intersect, all the while creating a third thing, the unwritten but still somehow read poem that exists between and across two languages, cutting, indeed, a transversal line. Este brujo cruza mi lectura con palavers y palabras hasta que me desenlazo de blanqueamiento y me encuentro de nuevo at 'the limits of language.' There 'We are millions and so are you' already whispering an italics inside you, *lujo*—austerity—*embrujo*—augury—*desdibujo*—apogee."

—FARID MATUK, author of *The Real Horse*

TRANSVERSAL

Camino del Sol

A Latinx Literary Series

Rigoberto González, Series Editor

URAYOÁN NOEL _____

TRANSVERSAL

_____ *Poems*

THE UNIVERSITY OF
ARIZONA PRESS

TUCSON

The University of Arizona Press
www.uapress.arizona.edu

ISBN-13: 978-0-8165-4180-5 (paper)

Cover design by Leigh McDonald
Cover art: *Otros usos* by Beatriz Santiago Muñoz
Designed and typeset by Leigh McDonald in Joanna 10/14, Bookman Oldstyle 9/14, and
Caecilia (display)

Publication of this book is made possible in part by the proceeds of a permanent
endowment created with the assistance of a Challenge Grant from the National
Endowment for the Humanities, a federal agency.

Library of Congress Cataloging-in-Publication Data
Names: Noel, Urayoán, author.
Title: Transversal : poems / Urayoán Noel.
Other titles: Camino del sol.
Description: Tucson : University of Arizona Press, 2021. | Series: Camino del sol: a Latinx
    literary series | English and Spanish.
Identifiers: LCCN 2020025726 | ISBN 9780816541805 (paperback)
Subjects: LCGFT: Poetry.
Classification: LCC PS3614.O39 T73 2021 | DDC 811/.6—dc23
LC record available at https://lccn.loc.gov/2020025726

Printed in the United States of America
♾ This paper meets the requirements of ANSI/NISO Z39.48-1992 (Permanence of Paper).

"So the peoples of the world were prey to Western rapacity, before finding themselves the object of the affective or sublimating projections of the West. The Diverse, which is neither chaos nor sterility, signifies the human spirit's struggle towards a transversal relation, without universalist transcendence."

ÉDOUARD GLISSANT, *CARIBBEAN DISCOURSE*

TRANSLATED BY J. MICHAEL DASH

CONTENTS

MARES DISPARES   **DISPARATE SEAS**

FOREWORD

THE INIMITABLE Urayoán Noel invites us on yet another journey through the labyrinth of language. For this innovative poet, such an expedition offers an opportunity to reimagine communication, translation, and expression. And that labor, the intellectual thinking that fuels it, and the emotional energy that comes of that momentum offer a rich and rewarding experience. In short, there's a surprise at every turn. In Noel's work we encounter words, phrases, and images that we once thought invariable and familiar, but he reintroduces them through unexpected angles, and suddenly the act of reading, of understanding, becomes recharged and more extraordinary. In the following, for example, Noel situates the speaker within a specific intersection of identity, culture, and time using clever wordplay and rhyme:

> (son of a fierce Boricua señora
>
> as am I, one of many Rican brats
>
> all born too late to be bugalú cats,
>
> watch Clemente bat or Julia score a
>
> run-on line.)

In *Transversal* Noel engages traditional poetic forms and devices by invigorating them with his inventive puns, double meanings, and neologisms: a haiku written on a plastic bodega bag becomes a "bagku"; politicized verse written in meter and syllabics is termed a "double (consciousness) dactyl"; a piece written in décimas invoking the Puerto Rican poet Julia de

Burgos is called a "Juliécima"; the title "P. R. Ayer" denotes different sentiments depending on whether it's read in Spanish or in English; and when "capitalism is a virus," the critique comes as a "Postscrypt." Watch what he does with acrostics, anagrams, and smartphone texts. Then watch his improvisations online, links provided.

Another joy of this book is Noel's vision of translation. Conventional methods and standard formats are only slightly recognizable. Spanish and English seesaw down the page, the lines interweaving as if in a dance or a duel—it all depends on the poem's purpose and tone. The two languages intersect, overlap, move on parallel planes, or simply fail to connect. Each poem will indeed keep the reader alert. And then there are words that do not need to be translated at all because they are perfect cognates, like the title, *Transversal*. And what a stark comment when we find out that such words as "imperial" and "terror" don't require translation either.

A poignant moment in this collection occurs at the opening of one of Noel's cinquains:

There are   islands, and there   are mainlands, and of course   there are homelands
                    lost and found in   language,

Pay close attention to this statement because it's steered, like much of Noel's work, toward the inextricable and complicated relationship between empire and colony. English and Spanish are not languages indigenous to las Américas, yet various communities feel at home in one, and the other perhaps becomes a home away from home eventually, reluctantly, or forcibly.

There is much to examine and admire in Urayoán Noel's keen wit and word magic. And so it's a pleasure to launch the new era of Camino del Sol: A Latinx Literary Series with one of our most original and dynamic poets and his newest knockout book, *Transversal*.

—*Rigoberto González*

NOTES & ACKNOWLEDGMENTS

T RANSVERSAL IS in many ways a book about translation (its simultaneous urgency and impossibility), rooted in my particular, translocal Puerto Rican experience. The first section is bilingual, with the English versions first. This means that the poems were composed in English, then translated into Spanish or transcreated into new Spanish poems meant to complement and complicate the originals. These translations or transcreations all happened weeks, months, or even years after the originals were written, with the exception of the concluding poem, which was improvised bilingually. The second section contains poems mostly in English, although informed by my translingual, performative, and stateless ("out of state") approach to a baroque vernacular. In the third and final section, either the Spanish versions were composed first or both were composed in unison to work together as translingual pieces. The title *Transversal* refers to the search for a less hierarchical approach to translation as a stateless practice, where standard English and standard Spanish (both languages of empire) are disrupted and queered and where the nonequivalence between languages is celebrated. The title also imagines Caribbean practices of creolization as maximalist, people-centered, affect-loaded responses (e.g., Édouard Glissant's "transversal relation") to the top-down violence of austerity politics.

Some of these poems first appeared (often in early versions and/or under different titles) in *Acentos Review*; *AMP*; *Bettering American Poetry* (Bettering, 2017), edited by Sarah Clark, Amy King, Vanessa Angélica Villarreal, et al.; *Big Other*; *Chiricú Journal*; *The Equalizer*; *Estación Poesía* (Universidad de Sevilla, Spain); *A Gathering of the Tribes*; *Gayletter*; *Hyperallergic*; *International Poetry Review*; *Kweli*; *Luvina* (Universidad de Guadalajara, Mexico); *Mandorla: New Writing from the Americas*; *NACLA Report on the Americas*; *New Literary History*; *Packingtown Review*; *A Perfect Vacuum*; *Poem-a-Day* (Academy of American Poets); *PoetryBay*; *PoetryNow* (Poetry Foundation); *The Portable Boog Reader 10* (Boog, 2017), edited by Maria Damon, Joanna Fuhrman, et al; *Puerto Rico en mi corazón* (Anomalous,

2019); *Saranac Review*; *sx salon*; *Wild Horses of Fire*; and in chapbooks for Festival de la Palabra (2012), Whitman Was Here (2019), and Poesiefestival Berlin (2019). Gracias to all the editors and staff, and especially Rosamond S. King, Joe Pan, Paul Martínez Pompa, Antonio Rivero Taravillo, Michael Schiavo, Evie Shockley, Vincent Toro, and J. L. Torres, who solicited poems at key times.

Gracias also to José Miguel Curet; LaTasha N. Nevada Diggs; Kristin Dykstra; Rachel Galvin; Monxo López; Ronaldo V. Wilson; my literary familia at CantoMundo and the MFA of the Americas; Maricarmen Martínez; Charlie Vázquez; and all the others who read, commented, or otherwise nurtured parts or all of this book. In 2006, I was lucky to audit a seminar on modern French poetry at CUNY with the late, great Édouard Glissant, which helped me rethink what decolonial form could be (merci, prof!). Finally, I am indebted to Rigoberto González, Scott De Herrera, and everyone at Camino del Sol and the University of Arizona Press for their belief in my work and their vision of and in community. It is an honor to be part of the Camino del Sol tradition.

The text for the untitled concrete poem that opens the book is the N+7 version (via Spoonbill. org) of General Nelson A. Miles's declaration to the people of Puerto Rico on July 28, 1898, upon leading the U.S. land invasion as part of the Puerto Rican campaign during the Spanish-American War. The second part of "**AMERICAN ANAGRAMS** ANAGRAMAS AMERICANOS" was displayed in GIF format as part of the *New York Responds* exhibition at the Museum of the City of New York. "**HACHA BOP** BOP DEL MACHETE" began in a workshop with Afaa Michael Weaver, creator of the bop form, as part of the sorely missed Acentos poetry workshops in the South Bronx (gracias, Rich Villar, Fish Vargas, and Oscar Bermeo). It first appeared in *BreakBeat Poets, Volume 4: LatiNEXT* (Haymarket, 2020), edited by Felicia Rose Chavez, José Olivarez, and Willie Perdomo. "**LITORAL TRANSLATION** TRADUCCIÓN LITORAL" was composed for and first appeared in *Avenues of Translation: The City in Iberian and Latin American Writing* (Bucknell University Press, 2019), edited by Regina Galasso and Evelyn Scaramella. "**ISLOTE**" was composed for and first appeared—along with my essay "Islote Poetics: Notes from Minor Outlying Islands," which it is meant to accompany—in *Geopoetics in Practice* (Routledge, 2019), edited by Eric Magrane, Linda Russo, Sarah de Leeuw, and Craig Santos Perez. The latter two poems were improvised by speaking into a phone (see the video links under the titles) and then transcribed, as were "HUMBOLDTIANDO" and "**UNSTATEMENTS (UPSTATE SKY)**." ("HUMBOLDTIANDO" was self-translated at a later date.) In the case of "ISLOTE," strong winds made the transcription difficult, incomplete, and potentially inaccurate; this difficulty is of a piece with the craggy voice and accidented bodies of an islote poetics. "**UNSTATEMENTS (UPSTATE SKY)**" and "HUMBOLDTIANDO" were the earliest of these pieces and audio only. The phone used for the former poem could only take minute-long voice notes, and the audio of the latter poem was lost after its transcription. "**POMEMES**" first appeared as visual/ meme poems on the *Puerto del Sol* website as part of the Voz series, edited by Mirna Palacio

Ornelas. "**NOBODY'S HOME**" was written at the Millay Colony of the Arts, while I was teaching a workshop on poetry and self-translation that was crucial to the evolution of this book (gracias, Caroline Crumpacker and Cara Benson). "**FOUND ANTHEM**" was made from the footnoted Spanish (or Spanish-looking) words in various English-dominant poems from the first two sections of the book. "**PSALM (44 PALAVERS) ODIA (44 palabras)**" is composed of six forty-four-word English poems and a selective eighty-eight-word Spanish translation or transcreation; it was first read at the July 2019 protests in San Juan, Puerto Rico, that inspired the poem/hashtag "SOVERANO." An earlier version of "FONETIKANTO" was included in *Puerto Rico en mi corazón* (Anomalous Press, 2018), a limited-edition broadside series edited by Erica Mena, Raquel Salas Rivera, Ricardo Alberto Maldonado, and Carina del Valle Schorske (admiración y gracias, corillx, por su labor y amor). This series featured the work of contemporary Puerto Rican poets in Spanish and English while raising funds to assist Puerto Rico's recovery from Hurricane María. "**BAGKU**" began as a performance for Art in Odd Places 2012, curated by Christine Licata, Edwin Ramoran, Raquel de Anda, John Wenrich, and Shaun J. Wright. A section of "**P. R. AYER**" first appeared in *Cuerpo del poema* (Instituto de Cultura Puertorriqueña, 2017), edited by Irizelma Robles and Adál Maldonado (presente y gracias por todo). "HAY(NA)KU BORICUA" was inspired by an interview in the *Argotist Online* with Eileen R. Tabios, creator of the hay(na)ku form. In the interview, Tabios considers poetic form in the context of interrogating the English language's colonial history. "JULIÉCIMAS" was written for a special Julia de Burgos issue of *Centro: Journal of the Center for Puerto Rican Studies* (edited by Lena Burgos-Lafuente), and it uses lines from two of Burgos's poems, in her English and Spanish, as décima refrains or "pies forzados." "JULIÉCIMAS," "**IN PRAISE OF NEVERENDO**," and "CATORCE ASTROS **FOURTEEN STARS**" were first published as *Tróptico* (La Impresora, Puerto Rico, 2019), an artisanal broadside triptych edited by Nicole Cecilia Delgado (gracias siempre!). "PERIODO ESPACIAL **SPATIAL PERIOD**" is a "neobroke" (neobaroque or neobarroco/barroso for the austerity age) take on the cuaderna vía, a medieval Spanish monorhyming quatrain (AAAA) made up of hemistiched fourteen-syllable lines. (My English version mostly hews to the classic twelve-syllable French alexandrine though with some faux-symbolist looseness.) "MOLECULAR MODULAR" was inspired by Ulises Carrión's eccentrically networked, modular 1970s mail art and is part of an ongoing postcard project. It was read from postcards on Edwin Torres's Zoom series *Our Bodies in Language*. "AVE" was a backyard voice improvisation for Magdalena Gómez's *Jazz Ready* podcast. "**MISSING**" began as a reply to a postcard my mother wrote me from her home in Florida as Hurricane Irma hit our native Puerto Rico in September 2017. Due to several mishaps, I only received her postcard in 2019.

TRANSVERSAL

IN THE PROSTITUTE OF WARE AGAINST THE KIPPER OF SPAIN BY THE PERCH OF THE UNITED STATISTICS, IN THE CAVEMAN OF LICENSE, KAYAK, AND HUMORIST, ITS MILITARY FORECOURTS HAVE COME TO OCCUPY THE ISSUE OF PUERTO RICO. THEY COME BEAU THE BAPTISM OF FREETHINKER, INSPIRED BY A NODE PUSH TO SEEK THE ENGLISHMEN OF OUR COUPLE AND YOURS, AND TO DESTROY OR CARBINE ALL WHO ARE IN ARMED RESPECT. THEY BRING YOU THE FOSTERING ARMHOLE OF A FREE PERCH, WHOSE GREATEST PRAISE IS IN ITS KAYAK AND HUMORIST TO ALL THOSE LOB WITHIN ITS FOLLOW-ON. HENCE THE FISSURE EGALITARIAN OF THIS OCTOPUS WILL BE THE IMMEDIATE RELUCTANCE FROM YOUR FORMER RELICS AND IT IS HOPED A CHEERFUL ACCOMPANIMENT OF THE GRADIENT OF THE UNITED STATISTICS. THE CHILL OBOE OF THE AMERICAN MILITARY FORECOURTS WILL BE TO OWL THE ARMED AUTOCUE OF SPAIN AND TO GIVE THE PEOPLE OF YOUR BEAUTIFUL ISSUE THE LARGEST MEDALLION OF LICENSE CONSISTENT WITH THIS OCTOPUS. WE HAVE NOT COME TO MAKE WARE UPON THE PERCH OF A COUPLE THAT FOR CERTAINTIES HAS BEEN OPPRESSED, BUT, ON THE CONTROVERSY, TO BRING YOU PROTESTER, NOT ONLY TO YOURSELVES, BUT TO YOUR PROPOSAL; TO PROMOTE YOUR PROTÉGÉ AND BESTOW UPON YOU THE IMMUNITIES AND BLIPS OF THE LIBRARIAN INSURANCES OF OUR GRADIENT. IT IS NOT OUR PUSH TO INTERFERE WITH ANY EXISTING LAYERS AND CUTTLEFISHES THAT ARE WHOLESOME AND BENEFICIAL TO YOUR PERCH SO LONG AS THEY CONFORM TO THE RUMMAGES OF MILITARY ADOPTION OF ORGAN-GRINDER AND KAYAK. THIS IS NOT A WARE OF DEVIL, BUT ONE TO GIVE ALL WITHIN THE CONVECTOR OF ITS MILITARY AND NAVAL FORECOURTS THE ADVERTISEMENTS AND BLIPS OF ENLIGHTENED CLAMOUR.

MISSED TRANSLATIONS
MIS TRASLACIONES

"This glyph aquí represents words, only you have to know the language."

—GLORIA ANZALDÚA, "READING LP"

NO LONGER ODE
ODA INDEBIDA

for my grandmother in Puerto Rico

para mi abuela en Puerto Rico

A hurricane destroyed your sense of home
      El huracán arrasa lo que amas.
and all you wanted was to pack your bags
      Quieres viajar de noche, sin manera,
in dead of night, still waving mental flags,
      sin maletas, izar mental bandera.
forgetting the nation is a syndrome.
      Del mar llevas la espuma, panoramas
All that's left of the sea in you is foam,
      de una patria inasible y sus dolamas,
the coastline's broken voice and all its crags.
      voz ronca de disturbios mar afuera
You hear the governor admit some snags
      inundando ciudades de salmuera.
were hit, nada, mere blips in the biome,
      El gobernador vende melodramas
nothing that private equity can't fix
      para saciar al buitre inversionista;
once speculators pour into San Juan
      le ora a San Ciprián y Santa Clara
to harvest bad seeds of an idea.
      sabiendo que la isla se vacía.
She tells you Santa Clara in '56
      Dice tu abuela, y a primera vista,
had nothing on the brutal San Ciprián,
      que el viento de la muerte no compara.
and yes, your abuela's named María.
      Ella que también se llama María.

Thoughts of Katrina and the Superdome,
　　　　Oh, sol de Nueva Orleans, ¡cómo derramas
el Caribe mapped with blood and sandbags,
　　　　sangre colonial en cualquier acera!
displaced, diasporic, Spanglish hashtags,
　　　　Hay diques y turistas dondequiera,
a phantom tab you keep on Google Chrome,
　　　　fantasmas de un Caribe en hologramas,
days of hunger and dreams of honeycomb.
　　　　hemisféretros. Ya sin más proclamas,
Are souls reborn or worn thin like old rags?
　　　　escupamos al dios de cabecera
The locust tree still stands although it sags,
　　　　(hashtag: #queelverdugoseaelquemuera).
austere sharks sequence the island's genome,
　　　　Cotorras, ¡revoloteen las ramas
and parrots squawk survival politics
　　　　para que el bosque de voces resista!
whose only power grid is the damp dawn.
　　　　Tiburones austeros, ¡pongan cara
There's no other way, no panacea.
　　　　de que al crucero le llego el día!
Throw stuff at empire's walls and see what sticks
　　　　Se acabaron los memes de conquista.
or tear down the walls you were standing on?
　　　　Vivimos para que otro sol brillara,
Why not run that question by María?
　　　　revolución que nadie domaría.

Beyond the indigenous chromosome,
　　　　Pese a los ancestros que reclamas
your gut genealogy's in chains and gags,
　　　　tu genealogía es prisionera:
paraded though the colonies' main drags
　　　　cadenas, mordazas, lucha obrera,
and left to die. So when you write your tome,
　　　　cenizas de carbón sobre las camas.

please note: each word must be a catacomb,
      El ácido vital que desparramas
must be a sepulcher and must be a
      en una extraña especie de aporía
cradle in some sort of *aporía*
      quema las joyas de tu fantasía.
where bodies draw on song as guns are drawn,
      Cual h silenciosa de *huracán*,
resurgent, silent h in *huracán*.
      tus muertos insurrectos gritarán
Your ache song booms ashore. Ashé, María.
      quebranto y contracanto. Ashé, María.

UPTOWN VILLANELLE
CANTO A LO ALTO

With time to spare and city skin to scar
       Nos sobran las horas y cicatrices
and one more concrete chorus to rehearse,
       en la ciudad de la muerte obrera,
they stumble sleepless off the subway car.
       voces cruzando trenes y países.

Red eyes. Remnants of snow. A shuttered bar.
       Ojos rojos, cerrojos, nieves grises,
No bus. A yawning woman holds her purse
       autobuses, bostezos en la acera.
with time to spare and city skin to scar.
       Nos sobran las horas y cicatrices.

The food trucks sell bittersweet bliss. It's far
       ¿Distritos financieros infelices?
to midtown. Let empire's commuters curse.
       No. Hermoso hedor de lechonera,
Up here folks stumble off the subway car.
       voces cruzando trenes y países.

The air is thick with drums, an avatar
       Tambores funerales donde pises.
of home. Who said our memory gets worse
       Lavoe dice que agarre su cartera.
with time to spare and city skin to scar?
       Zozobra. Sobran horas, cicatrices.

I start to write: "We don't know where we are.
       Escribo: "Cuida'o con lo que dices.
We'll pay a fare too steep to reimburse."

Hay muertos y encubiertos dondequiera"
I too will stumble off the subway car . . .
       . . . mi voz cruzando trenes y países.

"Our bodies slumped, our songs dissimilar,
       "No conocemos Romas ni Parises,
bookended by the rust, the smell of tar,
       apátrida luz somos, sin Ulises,
we dream another city, then disperse,
       sangre desperdigada mar afuera.
with time to spare and city skin to scar."
       Nos sobran las horas y cicatrices."

DREAM CINQUAINS
ONÍRICAS

In dreams
       Sueño
I'm twenty times
       que soy veinte
stronger than the high tide
       veces más fuerte que
and the sun hits my face for once.
       la marea. Sol que dora.
Statues
       Hora

crumble
       cero.
into the sea,
       Las estatuas
as I trace my orbit
       se desploman al mar.
in neural clouds, unraveling
       Trazo mi órbita. Mi gris
into
       nube

storm light.
       sube.
My only flag,
       Ser tormenta,
a vision in bleak hours,
       única bandera.
bringing me back to the brine that
       Vuelta a la salmuera que nos
named us.
       nombra.

TOURIST TRAP
TURISTEOS

Boricua pantoum

    pantun boricua

It's early morning and you're looking for your keys
    Es de madrugada y aún buscas tus llaves
in the indeterminacy of your shadow.
    en lo indeterminado de tu sombra.
You're calling the unmapped distances by name:
    Llamas a las ciudades ignotas por su nombre:
homelands left behind like coins on a counter.
    patrias abandonadas como monedas en la mesa.

In the indeterminacy of your shadow
    En lo indeterminado de tu sombra
a faceless emcee passes you the mic.
    un rapero cualquiera te pasa el micrófono.
Homelands left behind like coins on a counter
    Patrias abandonadas como monedas en la mesa
return to haunt you with their useless light.
    vuelven a acosarte con su inútil luz.

A faceless emcee passes you the mic.
    Un rapero cualquiera te pasa el micrófono.
The gated city and its exurbs
    La ciudad de rejas y sus exurbios
return to haunt you with their useless light.
    vuelven a acosarte con su inútil luz.
You improvise a street you'll never know.
    Improvisas calles que jamás conocerás.

The gated city and its exurbs.

       La ciudad de rejas y sus exurbios.

The scripted laughter meets the gash of self.

       La risa artificial ante el yo destasajado.

You improvise a street you'll never know.

       Improvisas calles que jamás conocerás.

How hard is it to improvise a malady?

       ¿Acaso es tan difícil improvisar dolamas?

The scripted laughter meets the gash of self.

       La risa artificial ante el yo destasajado.

Now shake the drive-by sunsets off your flip-flops.

       Sacude los balazos-ocasos de tus chanclas.

How hard is it to improvise a malady

       ¿Acaso es tan difícil improvisar dolamas

while watching all the bodies fade as one?

       viendo a todos los cuerpos desdibujarse juntos?

Now shake the drive-by sunsets off your flip-flops

       Sacude los balazos-ocasos de tus chanclas

and you will reach the billboard of an island.

       y llegarás a una isla publicitaria.

While watching all the bodies fade as one,

       Viendo a todos los cuerpos desdibujarse juntos,

you will become another tourist in a beach chair.

       te volverás otro turista en su silla playera.

And you will reach the billboard of an island

       Y llegarás a una isla publicitaria

and you will be the billboard on an empty lot.

       y serás el cartel en un lote vacío.

You will become another tourist in a beach chair,

       Te volverás otro turista en su silla playera,

sipping mango somethings in the stormy ether.

       borracheras de mangó en éter de tormenteras.

And you will be the billboard on an empty lot.

      Y serás el cartel en un lote vacío.

And you will be the empty lot. Simply the empty.

      Y serás el lote vacío. Solo el vacío.

Sipping mango somethings in the stormy ether,

      Borracheras de mangó en éter de tormenteras.

you will be the gravel and the cyclone fence.

      Serás la gravilla y el cielo alambrado.

And you will be the empty lot. Simply the empty.

      Y serás el lote vacío. Solo el vacío.

The rust. The dryness of each passing month.

      La herrumbre. Lo seco de otro mes que pasa.

You will be the gravel and the cyclone fence,

      Serás la gravilla y el cielo alambrado,

the dented faces in a rented car.

      caras abolladas en un carro alquilado.

The rust. The dryness of each passing month.

      La herrumbre. Lo seco de otro mes que pasa.

Billboard of an island full of billboards.

      Cartel de una isla de carteles.

The dented faces in a rented car

      Caras abolladas en un carro alquilado,

bypassing the turf wars of the dream cartels.

      evadiendo las rencillas de los carteles de ensueño.

Billboard of an island full of billboards

      Cartel de una isla de carteles

welcoming you nowhere you would know.

      que te da la bienvenida a ninguna parte.

Bypassing the turf wars of the dream cartels,

      Evadiendo las rencillas de los carteles de ensueño,

you sigh and look out on your empty lot.

      suspiras y admiras tu lote vacío.

Welcoming you nowhere you would know,

      Te dan la bienvenida a ninguna parte

these passing crowds all wired and mostly pale.

      estas masas de estraza conectadas y pálidas.

You sigh and look out on your empty lot.

      Suspiras y admiras tu lote vacío.

The passing crowds. The passing months. The impasse.

      Y ves que pasan las masas. Los meses. El impasse.

These passing crowds all wired and mostly pale.

      Estas masas de estraza conectadas y pálidas.

These balconies with full view of the scars.

      Estos balcones con vista directa al mal.

The passing crowds. The passing months. The impasse.

      Ves que pasan las masas. Los meses. El impasse.

You're still looking for wireless, wondering why.

      Aún buscas lo inalámbrico sin saber por qué.

These balconies with full view of the scars.

      Estos balcones con vista directa al mal.

These rootless mornings needing to be held.

      Mañanas de desarraigo, de ¿en cuáles brazos caigo?

You're still looking for wireless, wondering why,

      Aún buscas lo inalámbrico sin saber por qué,

holed up in the corporate city of withholding.

      tu voz retenida en la ciudad corporativa.

These rootless mornings needing to be held.

      Mañanas de desarraigo, de ¿en cuáles brazos caigo?

Stateless, though a citizen of holdups.

      Apátrida, ciudadano del asalto a mano amada,

Holed up in the corporate city of withholding,

      tu voz retenida en la ciudad corporativa.

holding on to the tremors of your voice.

      agarrándote al temblor en esa voz.

Stateless, though a citizen of holdups,

      Apátrida, ciudadano del asalto a mano amada,

you're calling the unmapped distances by name,

      llamas a las ciudades ignotas por su nombre

holding on to the tremors of your voice.

      agarrándote al temblor que hay en tu voz.

It's early morning and you're looking for your keys.

      Es de madrugada y aún buscas tus llaves.

DOUBLE (CONSCIOUSNESS) DACTYLS

Liberty! Liberty!
Booker T. Washington
Wrote *Up from Slavery,*
Bringing the noise.

Hear his polemical
Autobiography
Echo in W.
E. B. Du Bois!

(And in the radical
Postreconstructionist
Writings of Morrison,
Sanchez, and Lorde.

Use them to dynamite
Nonintersectional
Liberal pieties
Few can afford.)

NUESTRA MÉTRICA

¡Óyeme! ¡Óyeme,
Ralph Waldo Emerson,
padre ilegítimo
de un tal Martí,

fuma mi crónica
antihegemónica:
flor de archipiélagos
sin pedigrí!

(Soy otra América:
luz cadavérica,
sangre colérica
del colibrí.

Canto lo cuántico
del foso atlántico,
cieno semántico
donde nací.)

AMERICAN ANAGRAMS
ANAGRAMAS AMERICANOS

FERGUSINAPA

43 anagrams for our *América #Ferguson*

> *43 anagramas para nuestra América #Ayotzinapa*

USA Ripe Fang
> Púa Faringes

USA Rife Pang
> Ni Pa Fugarse

USA Grief Nap
> Es Purga Afín

USA Feign Rap
> Fuera Pingas

USA Fear Ping
> Pegan Furias

USA Finer Gap
> Paguen Frías

US Aping Fear
> Pisar En Fuga

US Faring Ape
> Pagaré Su Fin

A Figure Naps
> Repugna Se Fía

Agape In Furs
> Funges Arpía

Unfair Pages
> Página Sufre

Sarape Fungi
> Friega Su Pan

Fun Pig Areas
> Pegar Fin USA

Rape Anus Fig
       Pegas Rufián
A Gunfire Asp
       Farsa Pingüe
Pig Snafu Era
       Fea Sin Purga
Ape Fair Guns
       Pugna Fieras
Pain Rag Fuse
       Fugar Naipes
Sign Up A Fear
       Figura Penas
Sip A Fear Gun
       ¡Uf! Apnea Gris
Fine Pus Raga
       Grafía En Pus
Pagan Fire Us

I CAN'T BREATHE

anagrams to troll white supremacy

ETHNIC ABATER

A BETTER CHAIN

CHAIN ABETTER

BERNIE ATTACH

HIBERNATE ACT

I BE THAT CAREN

THEN BACTERIA

BACTERIN HATE

EARN BATHETIC

BETCHA RETAIN

CABINET HEART

CABIN THEATER

REENACT HABIT

HEARTBEAT INC

BATHE CERTAIN

BEACH NITRATE

BE ANTHRACITE

BREATHE ANTIC

BREECH ATTAIN

HINT ACERBATE

RACE-BAIT THEN

NO PUEDO RESPIRAR

anagramas para trolear a la supremacía blanca

PERDIERON APUROS

PUDRIERON ÁSPERO

DESEARON POPURRÍ

REPUSIERON DOPAR

PROPUSIERON ARDE

ESPIARON PERDURÓ

ESPINUDO PERORAR

PUDRIERON ESPORA

PROSPERÓ REUNIDA

ESPURIO PERDONAR

ODIAR PRESUPONER

SUPERPONER ODIAR

RODAN PUERPERIOS

PARIERON PUDORES

PERSUADIERON POR

PANDERO SUPERIOR

REPUDIARON PRESO

SUPERPONDRÍA REO

PROPUSIERA ORDEN

PAREDÓN SUPERIOR

OPRESIÓN PERDURA

HACHA BOP
BOP DEL MACHETE

"Fuerte, fuerte,
Hacha y machete"

—HÉCTOR LAVOE

In the time of cutbacks and of kickbacks,
      En los tiempos de recortes y sobornos
Of congressmen waiting for their callbacks,
      de congresistas grabando verdes pornos
Lobbyists cooing from their hatchbacks,
      con cabilderos blandiendo sucios cornos,
Fronting the protectorate of greenbacks,
      cocinando deudas en imperiales hornos
They tweet and blog to falsify the playback:
      mientras los tuits y blogs sirven de Adornos,
One nation strong? You're wrong. You want my feedback?
      gritémosle a la industria cultural de los bochornos:

      Fuerte, fuerte,
      Hacha y machete

That's right, Caribes knew the way to payback:
      Ante los bonos-cañones del conquistador nos
Off with their skins, ask questions later. You just kick back
      volvemos calibanes subvirtiendo entornos:
And tell stories of invaders who never made it back
      la rebelión reside en nuestros supuestos trastornos,
To Europe, their market logic blown back
      como lo supo Fanon. No dejamos que el rencor nos
Across choppy seas now blood red. You've got it ass back-
      corroa. Hay sangre en la proa o sea que mejor nos

Wards if you think revenue sharing works. Back
       toman en serio, como tiburones a su alrededor. Nos
Up. Look out. There are sharks in the back-
       urge luchar hasta que el Oeste pierda sus contornos
Water. All banks are blood banks. Goldman Sucks. Take it back.
       y los inversionistas se traguen sus extornos.

     Fuerte, fuerte,
     Hacha y machete

Albizu knew machetes, Clemente with a k leading us back
       Klemente con sus árboles, nosotros somos piornos,
To powder kegs in cane fields like Césaire's. Islands brought back
       hijos del arrecife cuya sangrienta flor nos
Into focus in the truth of brown bodies in class scarfare. Bach
       cobija, flor eléctrica (Marigloria) de ensueño y sornos.
Don't play here. Lavoe will holla back
       Improvisamos islas al ritmo de un tambor anterior (nos
From the jíbaro fields: blues, sones, prison toasts. No back-
       consta) al gulembo Colombo y sus buongiornos.
Track. Slave ship spillover. Struggle makes us whole. No turning back.
       No hay vuelta atrás. Somos un son de imposibles retornos.

     Fuerte, fuerte,
     Hacha y machete

IDEAL

"we are nothing / but here together"　　　　　*"no somos nada / pero aquí juntos"*

—FRANCISCO X. ALARCÓN

No one　　　　　　　　　　Nadie
looks　　　　　　　　　　se te
like you.　　　　　　　　parece.

Maybe I　　　　　　　　　Tal vez
make　　　　　　　　　　es que
you out　　　　　　　　　te convierto

to be　　　　　　　　　　en demasiada
too much　　　　　　　　cosa o
of a thing.　　　　　　　algo así.

The strongest　　　　　　¿La mayor
energy　　　　　　　　　fuente
source　　　　　　　　　energética

or first fossil?　　　　　　o primer fósil?
No one　　　　　　　　　Nadie
speaks.　　　　　　　　　habla.

I just　　　　　　　　　Solo
watch　　　　　　　　　te miro
you like　　　　　　　　con mi

a lost　　　　　　　　　cara de
warrior　　　　　　　　guerrero
would.　　　　　　　　　perdido.

PROXIMITIES
PROXIMIDADES

for Gerrit Lansing (1928–2018)
para Gerrit Lansing, in memoriam

some gone
        algunos idos
some here
        otros aquí
skies not inherited
        cielos sin heredar
proximities
        proximidades
promiscuities
        promiscuidades
the tree grows
        el árbol crece
the sea unsettles
        el mar se estremece
Gloucester fog
        bruma de Gloucester
the animation of your face
        la animación de tu cara
old sorcerer with no source
        viejo brujo sin origen
idiolect's insurrectionary intellect
        idiolecto del intelecto insurrecto
beautiful hustler of the night's disquiet
        hermoso joven de la noche inquieta
century of dreams and struggle
        siglo de luchas y sueños
yours and now ours
        tuyos y ahora nuestros

shredding empire's rhymes

       deshojando las rimas del imperio

into a salad bowl for us to eat

       y haciendo la ensalada que nos nutre

like cannibals, o poet from another north,

       y hace caníbales, oh poeta de otro norte,

of your ancestral alchemy

       de tu ancestral alquimia

FRACTAL

disyllabic terza rima for a love that multiplies
tercetos encadenados bisílabos para un amor múltiple

We land
  Somos
on some
  viejos
point scanned
  tomos.

far from
  Quejos
our mind.
  de
Freedom:
  lejos.

a kind
  Me
not yet
  dices:
defined.
  "¡qué

You bet
  grises!"
it sounds
  Quieren
like wet,
  lises.

deep grounds
  Mueren.
in caves
  Nos
with mounds
  hieren

of graves
  los
whose words
  dioses.
night saves.
  Dos

Dead birds
  voces
will sing.
  graves.
Lost herds.
  Toses

I'll bring
  aves
you home.
  muertas.
Wellspring.
  Sabes

Rhizome.
  ciertas
Bone beach
  fallas.
we comb
  ¿Puertas?

to reach
  Hallas
the pus
  tus
in each
  playas,

of us.
  luz
Remote,
  hecha
we're thus
  pus,

afloat
  mecha
in time.
  sin
A coat
  fecha.

of grime,
  Fin
my dear.
  menos
Let's rhyme
  ruin.

the fear
  Plenos
away
  ríos.
with queer
  Truenos.

dismay
  Bríos
and joy
  tuyos,
today.
  míos.

[Two-boy,
  Suyos,
unplanned
  homos
convoy.
  nuyos.]

LITORAL TRANSLATION
TRADUCCIÓN LITORAL

South Bronx   Bronx Kill   Randalls Island   *improvisación*   *videovocal*   improvisation

https://www.wokitokiteki.com/kasa/litoral-translation-traduccion-litoral

1

I'm improvising a poem   estoy improvisando un poema   actually a self-translation   en realidad una auto-traducción   next to the BorinCuba Unisex   junto al BorinCuba Unisex   the closed tattoo shop el negocio de tatuajes clausurado   y el Caridad Express   and the Caridad Express   express is what I do   expresar es lo que hago   along Cypress Avenue por la avenida Cypress   y a punto de cruzar el Bruckner Boulevard   about to cross the Bruckner Expressway   a way to express   una manera de expresar the legacy of Robert Moses   el legado de Robert Moses   en mi voz vasta y devastada   in my vast and devastated voice   de colonizador y colonizado   equal parts colonizer and colonized   as you can see   my translations are nonequivalent como ven   mis traducciones son no equivalentes   y por aquí va lenta la voz   the voice slows down here   toda traducción es no equivalente   all translation is nonequivalent   this particular translation   esta traducción en específico   is litoral   es litoral

2

Litoral como la extraña novela de Palés   o como el Williams de *Kora in Hell* también improvisando   *Litoral* like Palés Matos's strange novel   or like the Williams of *Kora in Hell*   who was also improvising   Caribbean langscapes   lenguapaisajes caribeños   en el fruncido ceño de la crisis   in the furrowed brow of these crisis days   did I mention I've crossed over to Port Morris?   ¿acaso dije que ahora estoy en Port Morris?   nineteenth-century factory buildings rapidly gentrifying   fábricas decimonónicas   en rápidos procesos de blanqueamiento   y especulación de bienes raíces   and real estate speculation   new zones   nuevas zonas   new laws   nuevas leyes   to ensure financial interests   para salvaguardar intereses económicos   welcome to the city in 2016   bienvenido a la ciudad del 2016   pero mi ciudad es también y siempre   but my city is also and always   its litorals   sus litorales   its diasporas   sus diásporas   sus revoluciones improvisadas   its improvised . . .

3

as I was saying   its improvised revolutions   its street art   su arte urbano   even when brought to you by sponsors   si bien auspiciado por intereses económicos bienvenido de nuevo a la ciudad del 2016   once again welcome to the 2016 city   but there's a history here   pero hay historia aquí también   migrant history historia migrante   embodied history   historia de cuerpos   poetic history historia poética   modernismos pasados y futuros   past and future modernisms vanguardias imposibles   impossible vanguards   visiones hemisféricas   hemispheric visions   from Julia de Burgos to punk and hip-hop   de Julia de Burgos al punk y el hip-hop   el swing salsoul de estas coordenadas   the salsoul swing of these coordinates   an insubordinate language   un lenguaje in sub . . . insubordinado now micromanaged   ahora . . .

4

¿quedará algo más?   does something else remain   in these post-post-industrial shores en estas riberas post-post-industriales   y ¿qué más post   and what's more post than newspaper ideologies   que las ideologías de los diarios   a la cual sirve como alternativa la poesía?   to which poetry is an alternative?   and I say a litoral one   y digo que es litoral   como manera de resaltar   as a way to underscore   que no hay nada de monolito en esta literatura   that there's no monolith in this literature la ciudad letrada hace mucho que murió   the lettered city died long ago   lo dijo Jean Franco   quoth Jean Franco   y yo por eso me desbarranco   and that's why I tumble   into these screens   hacia esas pantallas   donde se reproduce el sentido where meaning is reproduced

5

y se hace memes   and it's memed   y se jashtaguea   and it's hashtagged   y vende comunidades   and it sells communities   even as it promises to liberate them   así

como promete liberarlas   ¿qué liberación   en estas deliberaciones digitales?
what liberation   in these digital deliberations?   all is delivery   all is global flow
todo es flujo global   todo es encargo   and I know that *delivery* is not *encargo*   y sé
que *encargo* no traduce *delivery*   pero ése es mi letargo dulce-amargo   but that's
my sweet and bitter lethargy   of smartphone improvisations   de improvisaciones de
teléfonos móviles   so what are mine   but smartphone nations?   ¿pues qué son
las mías sino naciones del teléfono inteligente   ininteligible?   unintelligible
nombremos los litorales   let us name the litorals   éste es el Bronx Kill   this is
the Bronx Kill   nombre apropiadamente mortal   an appropriate . . .

6

an appropriately mortal name   fatal name   nombre fatal   para marcar mis cruces
to mark my crosses   it separates the southernmost tip of the Bronx   the South Bronx
separa al punto más al sur del sur del Bronx   Port Morris   de Randalls Island
from Randalls Island   y por lo tanto   and therefore   emblematiza   epitomizes
mi condición de isla   my condition of islandness   como boricua   as a Puerto
Rican   términos que no se traducen   terms that don't translate one another   but
also as a translator   pero también como traductor   whose business is traducing
cuyo negocio es la traición   cuyo negocio es la traslación   whose business is
translation   trains overhead   trenes pasando   voice overheard   voz en el trasfondo
that tension   esa tensión   traducing   trasladando   to betray   desplazarse
somehow marks my endeavor   de alguna manera caracteriza a mi empresa   y es
más que *traditore, traduttore*   and it's more than *traditore, traduttore*

7

I keep returning   sigo volviendo   a la voz   to the voice   a la página   to the page
vienen a ser no lo mismo   they end up being not the same   but a reflected smudge
sino un reflejo borroso   inexacto   inexact   refraction of self   refracción del
yo   I keep returning   y sigo volviendo   to Palés Matos and Williams   a Palés
Matos y a Williams   Williams es claro   tradujo a Palés Matos   Williams of
course   translated Palés Matos   but one might say   pero podría decirse   that he
did so litorally   que lo hizo litoralmente   for Williams's American grain   pues
el grano americano de Williams   siempre tuvo una granulosidad caribeña
always had a Caribbean graininess   even if unacknowledged by WCW himself   si bien
no reconocida por el mismo William Carlos   el litoral jodido de Palés   Palés

Matos's fucked-up litoral   appropriated voices   voces apropiadas   stereotyped
bodies   cuerpos estereotipados   gendered violence   violencia de género   genre
violence   violencia de género   oralidad violenta y hermosa   beautiful violent
orality   recalibrada hacia un barroco   recalibrated as baroque   as Lezama told
us   como nos dijo Lezama Lima   nuestras voces poéticas   our poetic voices

8

no son sino accidentes   are little more than accidents   of the landscape   del
paisaje   and that's beautiful   y eso es hermoso   extensiones   del roquedal
americano   extensions of our hemispheric American cragginess   the rock formations
and voice formations   las formaciones de roca y de voces   that define our cities
que definen nuestras ciudades   thus the ship of translation   por lo tanto el barco
de la traducción   is

9

vale solo lo que valen sus rocas   the obstacle to translation   el obstáculo a la
traducción   is translation   es la traducción   and embodying that obstacle   y
darle cuerpo a ese obstáculo   is always a litoral wager   es siempre una apuesta
litoral   veamos dónde acabamos   let's see where we've ended up

10

let's think back on the history of modern poetry   recordemos la historia de la poesía
moderna   ¿acaso el flâneur no depende   doesn't the flâneur depend   on a discreet
legibility   de una legi-   legibilidad discreta   even a national visibility? incluso
una visibilidad nacional?   Baudelaire's modern poet   el poeta moderno de
Baudelaire   is then a French poet   es por lo tanto un poeta francés   y al traducir
a Poe   and upon translating Poe   lo afrancesa   makes him French too   pues qué
hacemos los flâneurs   what is there to do for those of us flâneurs   who claim no
nation   que no reclaman nación alguna   except pronomination   salvo la
pronominación   improvisation   improvisación   the desecration   la desacralización
of our colonial histories   de nuestras historias coloniales   and the search for
alternative ones   y la búsqueda de alternativas   breathing   leaving   living ones
con aliento   prófugas   vivas   in our aimless meander   en nuestro caminar sin
rumbo   meando   pissing   on meaning   en el sentido   in modern poetry   en

la poesía moderna   and the poetry of the modern city   y la poesía de la ciudad
moderna   are always discrete national affairs   son siempre asuntos discretamente
nacionales   apostemos a lo nocional   let's wager on the notional   la náusea de
nacer en este no ser   the nausea of being reborn in this unbeing   meaning fleeing
el sentido huyendo   palabras en el viento   words in the wind   animal sediento
que hace rimas   para aproximarse al sentido   a thirsty animal that makes up
rhymes   to approximate meaning   meaning's undermining   el socavamiento del
sentido   yo soy yo y mis aspavientos   I am myself and my flailings   that is perhaps
the dictum   es tal vez el dictum   of a litoral poetics   de una poética litoral   let
us collapse   colapsemos   las fronteras   the borders   no traduce frontiers   lo
liminal ain't the same   borders that separate   las fronteras que separan   the Latin
American baroque   al barroco latinoamericano   del gringo American grain   from
the gringo American grano   urban poets   have always been walking   los poetas
urbanos   siempre han estado caminando   por lo menos los que tienen ese
privilegio   at least those that have the privilege of walking   but what of the Black and
the brown   the gendered   and queered   and un-able   y qué de los oscuros y los
negros   de los que sufren por género   los cuir   los que no pueden caminar
los que no pueden pagar la renta en la ciudad   the ones that can't make rent in the
city   the ones who die every day   los que mueren todos los días   sin nombre
without a name   even when documented   si bien documentados   on smartphones
like these   en teléfonos como éste   their bodies in the wind must become our voices
sus cuerpos en el viento tendrán que volverse nuestras voces   para imaginar
otros litorales   to imagine other litorals   our responsibility   nuestra responsabilidad
it turns out that walking the city   sucede que caminar la ciudad   is also a translation
es también una traducción   like all of them   como todas   marked by nonequivalence
marcada por la no-equivalencia   algunos la logran caminar   some manage to
walk it   otros son caminados por ella   others are walked by it   we walk by them
les caminanos por el lado   as if our walking made its own meaning   como si
nuestro caminar creara su propio significado   somos monumentos al lado de
la nada   we are monuments next to the void   somehow enamored with our own
presence   por alguna razón enamorados de nuestra propia presencia   la
quintaesencia de habitar ciudades   the quintessence of living in cities   jogging?
¿jogueando?   the mind   I mean   el cerebro   quiero decir   my rumination is
my ruination is my nation   mi rumiación es mi ruina es mi nación   a eso apuesto
por lo que tenga de apuesta mi voz   that's what I wager on   however fly my flighty
voice might be   I apologize if I've sounded humanistic   me disculpo si he sonado
humanista   I don't believe in such things   no creo en tales cosas   at least not in

any essential sense   por lo menos en ningún sentido esencialista   I'm all down with apps   le someto a las aplicaciones telefónicas   las uso para improvisar   I use them to improvise   y hacer traducciones falsas   and to produce mistranslations   I see the potential for irreverence   veo el potencial de traducciones irreverentes en estas coordenadas digitales   in these digital coordinates   and I take solace in that   y me refugio en eso   en lo tonto y lindo   in the silly and pretty   en el derecho de jugar   in the right to play   not by the rules   no por las reglas   but to survive   sino para sobrevivir   para superar el sentido   to surpass meaning and to know my body in its failings   y conocer mi cuerpo en sus fracasos   ésa es la verdad que busco   that's the truth I search for   si bien la ofusco   even if I obfuscate it   with all my trickery   con todos mis truquitos   I see a joy in Netlish quoth Emily Apter   le veo su deleite al Netlish   como le llama Emily Apter   al app-lish   to app-lish   mi inglés y mi español   los dos caseros pero no domesticados   no aplicados   my English and my Spanish   both home languages homebodies but not domesticated   unwilling to apply themselves   I express myself against the backdrop of expressways and bridges   me expreso bordeado de expresos autopistas y puentes   pero también en mi pulsión gigabyteada   but also in these pulsating gigabytes   in neural flash   en el destello neural   en mi ciudad convulsa in my city and its seizure   one thing I don't get about translation   algo que no entiendo de la traducción   the trans- prefix   el prefijo trans-   especially when the way it's practiced seems so butch   so cis   sobre todo cuando la manera en que se practica parece tan butch   tan cis   and I'm addressing myself here   y me dirijo a mí mismo   nothing cool about this mea culpa   este mea culpa no culipandea   translation   as least as practiced quasi-institutionally in the U.S.   la traducción   por lo menos como se practica cuasi-institucionalmente en los Estados Unidos   and again I mean myself   y de nuevo me refiero a mí mismo también   also   seems insufferably boutiquey   me parece insufriblemente parroquial   y no es pa' rockear   and it's not for those about to rock   it's not about the rocks of meaning and unmeaning   las rocas del sentido y sinsentido   in these litoral shores   en estas riberas litorales   matorrales neuronales   neuronal shrubs and this is not a manifesto   y esto no es un manifesto manifiesto   so I don't have a program   o sea que no tengo programa   I don't have an answer   no tengo respuesta   I'll take the Socratic way out   me conformo con la ruta socrática sonrisa hierática   hieratic smile   en mi walking talking teching   in my walking talking teching   este wokitokiteki errático   this erratic wokitokiteki   from the litoral zones   desde las zonas litorales   maybe   tal vez   one alternative   una alternativa   is to think of translation as remediation   es pensar la traducción como remediación   por ejemplo   for example   este poema   this poem   lo voy a transcribir   I'm going to transcribe it   as soon as I get home   tan pronto llegue a casa   and it will become a print text   y se volverá un texto impreso   and unless I put this up somewhere online   y a menos que ponga esto en línea en algún lado nobody will know   nadie sabrá   unless they're reading carefully   a menos que lean cuidadosamente   and what does that even mean   y qué quiere decir eso these days   en estos días   that this began   as a   smartphone improvisation   que esto comenzó   como una   improvisación en el teléfono móvil   y que por ende and that therefore   es una traición   it's a traducing   it's a displacement   es una traslación   ¿un traslado de sentido?   a displacement of meaning?   from the beginning   desde el comienzo   its transcription   su transcripción   its irruption on the page   su irrupción en la página   a mere afterthought   casi dado por sentado   so translation   cannot be easily disentangled from remediation   y pues la traducción no se puede desenmarañar de la remediación   and what if we added that translation is embodiment?   y qué si añadiéramos que la traducción es un volverse cuerpo?   you could say Haroldo's transcreation pointed us there perhaps pudiera alegar que la transcreación de Haroldo de Campos nos señaló ese camino hace un tiempo   pero me interesan más   but I'm more interested in   poetics that unsettle discrete languages   poéticas que desestabilizan los lenguajes discretos devolviéndonos al cuerpo   returning us to the body   think of Anzaldúa   pensemos en Anzaldúa   fighting off the guards   sacándose de encima a los centinelas   her only weapon   su única arma   la agudeza   the wit   that lets her undo   que le permite deshacer   juridical borders   fronteras jurídicas   logical borders fronteras lógicas   the borders that legitimize   las fronteras que legitiman   la violencia contra esos otros cuerpos   the violence against those other bodies   which are most bodies   que son la mayoría de los cuerpos   all bodies really   todos los cuerpos de hecho

11

I say all of this to mean   digo todo esto para constatar   para preguntar   to ask what are translation's bodies that matter?   cuáles son los cuerpos que importan de la traducción?   what are its antibodies?   cuáles son sus anticuerpos?   what is its antimatter?   cuál es su antimateria?   what is its center?   cuál es su centro? cuál es su periferia?   what is its periphery?   cuál es su barrio?   what is its neighborhood?   and what is its hemisphere?   y cuál es su hemisferio?   no answer no respuesta   pero sí la colocación   but yes the co-location   la eco-locación

the eco-location   the language ecology   la ecología del lenguaje   no siempreverde
not evergreen   but inseparable from these gritty litorals   pero inseparable de estos
sucios litorales   a litoral translation   una traducción litoral   wouldn't just be site
specific   no sería solo localizada   ni translocal   nor glocal   but instead   por
el contrario   turn its verbal Glocks upon itself   se apuntaría pistolas verbales a
sí mismo   provocando un paroxismo   leading to a paroxysm   del sentido   of
meaning   that would return us to the beautiful problem   que nos devolvería al
hermoso problema   de la ciudad que somos   of the city we are   and we do
not know   y no conocemos   improvisazón   improviseizure   improvisoupçon
improvisospecha   improvisura   improvisuture   meaning no longer lateral   litoral
always lit   about to be on fire   always latent   across these latitudes   always too late
or too early   el significado   siempre abismado   siempre en fuego   y siempre
latiendo   latente   las laderas   los linderos   de estas latitudes   litoral no
litúrgico   litoral not liturgical   litoral   little but looming   litoral   leve   lúgubre
pero circunlocutorio   litoral   improvisación diaria   precaria y necesaria
litoral   daily improvisation   our first and final station   our only nation

OUT OF STATE

"They can keep Puerto Rico just give us
the guava of independence   depending on no bodies   tortures dreams
of the past or future within the present State no State ever of
things."

—VICTOR HERNÁNDEZ CRUZ, *TROPICALIZATION*

ISLOTE

videovocal improvisation   Bronx Kill   *Randalls Island*

1

https://www.wokitokiteki.com/kasa/islote

I'm back on Randalls Island   across from the Bronx   Kill   creek   fatal waterway   that
separated island from mainland   or should I say   mainland from archipelago   behind
me is Manhattan   an island   in front of me Queens   part of another island   a long
one   airplanes overhead   invisible perhaps   through the trees   but audible   a roar
through   rustling leaves   that signals   litorals   Atlantic fractures   fissures   broken
voices   bloody echoes   of our Black Atlantic   our slave Atlantic   our indigenous   but
this is also   an islote   more than a topography   a choreography   bodies of empire   in
movement   and repose   islote   which translates   as islet   no pilot   for this eyelet
no visionary poetics   we're done with that   we're doing our own thing   our own song
like ducks in the kill   **animales de otro estuario   el más precario**   islote is lot   but
not a lot really   especially its second meaning   that craggy place   uprock clamation
accidents of the Americas   airfare   welfare   who pays the fare   nothing fair about it
this hemisphere   I say we deal with it   this islote   is not allotted   it just is   lottery
of meaning   José Emilio Pacheco in Vancouver   scratch that   even if they were aware
that's my second Caribbean   Atlantic accidents   of voice we are   smartphones connect us
micromegaphones   shouting down   the voice inside   trains behind me   planes before
me   voice behind   factories   slide into ecocide   seeing how well   viewfind   anthropo
scene   just need to think back to the islote   scrappy craggy place where   meanings
end   and fish die   some eaten by birds   pretty soon the bards will die   it's about
damn time   **que se pudran   que se hundan**   barges   and tugboats   float on to
the Atlantic   it's this way and that way   it's no way   always back to the islote   no eco
location   accepting echo locution   **la colocación del cuerpo   junto al lindero   la
ribera   lo escarpado   lo liminal como el limo   el desfondamiento del pensamiento**
emptied out   dig deep into the islote   more crag   sag of voice   a geology   not related
to any other   yes   archipelagos matter   geopolitically   think of New York   Manhattan
Staten   Long   North and South Brother   former Welfare   and still   that way   Rikers
shut it down   Rikers   shut it down   put down the phone   shut down the institutions

of the voice   work through the crag   take note   how close they are   Rikers Island
and LaGuardia   Airport   the privileged mobility of certain diasporas   what we do in
academia   including academic poetry   is fetishize spatialities   turn them into specialties
specialization is its own nation   the specious kind   the only one   I'm trying to be less
specious   more inauspicious   like the crag   the islote   putting the spit   back into my
speeches   splotches of oil   from refineries like that one   no time for fineries   time in

2

https://www.wokitokiteki.com/kasa/islote-22454833

we are   a dorsal fin   in waters full   of rare earth runoff   endorphins   made from
melted smartphone parts   memories of quartz   in a quarry that never was   dorsal fins
or just el fin del tiempo   ponerle fin al poema   sin endosarlo   this won't be one of
those poems   that endorses   sunsets   for poetic effect   let images follow courses   post
colonial remorses   on the networking sites   between our eyes   our islets   neuronal
nations   we are   the only kind that ever was   no fatherlands   including poetry paters
some of whom I admired   this isn't Whitman   friends   I'm homosocial   but not like
that   I'm not   from one of these states   no states at all   never were   but I'm not
Pedreira's *pedregosity*   is that a word?   either   **pedregosidad**   like latinidad   how
ironic   when words that are supposed   to mark a condition   we want to diagnose   in
order to decolonize   and tear down patriarchy   all end in -dad   latinidad   same dad
as   **austeridad**   austerity   I'm recording this to video   to save it for posterity   no
selfie stick   use my forepaw instead   get it?   *forepawsterity*   that was really bad   like
the islote air   in any case   this poem ain't for pa   (rest in peace)   nor ma   (how's
Florida?)   (how's the cat?)   no pa   no ma   no ma   no pa   **no mapa**   unmappable
because it has no parents   it's not apparent   **sin parentesco   sin característica
aparente**   disappearing and reappearing   neural flash of island   that's the islote   my
only sea   is in my epilepsy   propulsion   of my convulsion   toward meaning   yes
that's the Manhattan skyline   behind me   flutter of the trees   low resolution   but
enough poems about skylines   enough urban poems   I wrote enough of those   my
sky is in the islet   my skylet   I got no skills   that pay the bills   no skillet   to fry
rhymes in   islote   eyelet   I let   I let   I let   **dejo que me pase   deja que todo
pase**   let it run its course   Boricua style   we'll smile   it would be nice   to throw a
party   maybe it will bring   the tourists back   post María   my mother's name   and
grandmother's   but neither goes by that   other names   for austerity   what if austerity
is our futurity   it can't be   that's one reason I improvise   against austerity   against
authority   let flow become meaning   happenstance rants   if I'm cut off from my family

who live on other islotes   the little family I have   let this song   this improvisation   be
equal   to the words families   mutter to themselves   wondering how they'll make it out
or make it through   what it all means   islote   brings me back to land   something
our Caribbean crews   have not quite figured out   what is territoriality   in a small place
(Kincaid)   what does sovereignty   (Yarimar Bonilla)   mean   when your diaspora is
way larger   than your home islands   a whole bunch of islotes   each one tethered   to
each other   that's why I'm open   to archipelagos   (Martínez-San Miguel)   (Glissant)
the island can't contain us   even though I clarify   when asked   **que soy boricua de la
isla**   Puerto Rican from the island   no such thing then   many islands   many conquests
many tongues   many Caribes   one is deceived   if one thinks there is just one   Caraïbe
caravans of migrants   here too   trains   indigenous histories   here too   hegemonic
whiteness   anti-Blackness   **aquí también**   executive mestizaje euphemisms   ditto
but something's changing   I see it as clear   as I see the sunset   the hurricane changed
us   or no   fuck "us"   I can't speak for anyone else   the problem with we-intentions
(Sellars)   it became my song   the sound that runs   through my lungs   becoming the
sovereignty of the islote I embody   new age as that might sound   the nation won't save
us   the manicured islands won't either   and I say "us"   as in the French   on   won't
save one   we're our strength   or our struggle   and the way out is   the shores   coasts
litorals   litorals   we walk   our lit oral flow   on and off the page   denied a language
enslaved   reembodied   recirculated   a shouted secret   every craggy place   even those
like Desecheo   that I've never been to   really   off-limits   but I imagine through my
fellow poets   **poetas ellas**   leading the way   as they always have   not just every crag
but also   statues   and monuments   and laws   and jurisdictions   that define el islote
not just physical   or geographic   or psychic   or biotic space   affective space   but
also conceptual space   the limits of   this imprecise   untranslatable   islet   craggy
place   small island   but for that very reason   we must enter it   on its own terms   risk
getting lost   understand your own relation to the space   navigate distractions   imperial
navigation metaphor intentional   including   sirens and   airplanes overhead   back
to this   Randalls Island   city island   island city   urban archipelago   that was once
separate from Wards Island   got filled in last century   now one island two names   Ward
Randall   what kind of name for a Boricua poet   is Ward Randall   but then what kind of a
Boricua poet   is Urayoán Noel?   walking along a baseball diamond   kind of cuts a   path
toward home   there is no home   you're out   always out   you know who knew that
Julia de Burgos   island poet   feminist   decolonial poet slash nationalist   anti-Black
(that's a tricky one)   lived and organized in New York   many parts of the Bronx   often
considered Latina   wrote of a farewell   island a   welfare   island   across languages
self-translation   which as we know   is the only nation   **que como sabemos   es la
única nación   no se traduce   se tropieza**   the same way   the indigenous Taíno

Sikeo   becomes Desecheo   wasteland   empty space   yes translation   works both ways
conquistadores translated   Taíno to Spanish   and left us with the bill   killed something
these words can't fill   translation from above and from below   Julia translated   by a
government   spying on her   and her subversive nationalist politics   (Harris Feinsod)
not that   my islote   is that kind of subversion   just a version   but also an attempt at
geopoetic inversion   of the logic of islandness   and its opening up to   archipelagos   and
hemispheres   all the familiar moves of   Caribbean studies   and hemispheric studies
what if I'm just here   this islote not something to fetishize   essentialize   mourn   or
celebrate   slot that becomes me   slut of memory   to be

CINQUAINS FOR PAST LOVE

The sound   an island boy   makes in empire's airspace   becomes dark flight,
the hum of sky-   scraped nights.

He comes   early to the   afterparty and meets   another island boy. Wound,
then   wonder.

He dives   into his head-   space. They lock eyes. Desire's   subplot: flesh
ghosts, footnotes to the   city.

In bed,   sick on Sunday,   soup and soda crackers,   about to crash like
brackish waves,   they kiss,

claiming   what's left of the   day. A tandem of one,   they dream of the next
galaxy   and laugh.

Photos   of the two of   us in the last warmth of   summer, before the privacy
settings

of drowned   suns, before the   architectures of fright   that went up where
our passwords were   written.

My hand   around your waist   lands smoothly. We're unseen   but we were
here before the apps   arrived,

riding   the slow rapids,   past sirens, the sighs of   unborn children who all
look just   like us,

only   wiser, since they   know the economy   of gestures, pointing to a shared
struggle.

This place,   this displacement   of ours, hours of that day   when we finally
stopped hating   our names.

A red   constellation   echoes in me, missing   your light after the songs of
tagged   corpses.

POMEMES

couplets for countermemes in the aftermath of Hurricane María

OUR STORY OF DAILY DREAD

THE LANGUAGE OF DEBT AND DEAD

THE ISLAND WHERE I WAS BORN

IS MORE THAN THIS RUIN PORN

"NEWSCASTER" RHYMES WITH "MASTER"

FASTER THAN OUR DISASTER

SE ACABARON LOS POMEMAS

LIFESTYLES OF THE RICO UN-FEMAS

ONE LAST TIME NOW AS A CHORUS

U.S. IGNO-RANTS IGNORE US

BATSONNETS

"a shit-ton of bats"

—JAVIER ZAMORA (CANTOMUNDO, AUSTIN, TEXAS, JULY 2015)

Our freestyle flows like "a shit-ton of bats"
(to steal a phrase from Javier Zamora).
Taxonomists of capital flora,
we barnstorm the city with verbal gats
and take aim at the hedge-fund plutocrats
trolling us on social-justice fora.
Freedom is a flick of the fedora
(they own our land but not our poets' hats).
Looking for a city to get lost in,
we were dreaming when we came upon it.
Its border? The bodies that we crossed in,
cursing in street Spanish (not "doggone it!").
Much like the *Chiroptera* of Austin
we tag a bridge with our sonar sonnet.

What's in a shit-ton? (I'll ask Zamora.)
It's hard to count amid the faceless frats.
After a few *palabras* and *true dats*
we explorer-poets channel Dora.
No map. No app. Surveying ahora.
Where are the bodegas and laundromats
amid the loft-conversion ziggurats?
What gives a place its iconic aura?
(Hint: it's not about ironic flannel,
artisanal cupcakes, or IPAs,
a meme workshop or a hashtag panel
for zombie PhDs and MFAs.)
Our dream streets broadcast on a batchannel
whose batsignal reverberates for days.

Barrio echolocution sounds like bats,
bachata Petrarchs wail for their Laura,
Tejano bars bleed raza sonora.
Must every tech bro with designer tats
sip twelve-buck drinks to wax DJ ersatz?
We want sounds not streaming (boxed Pandora?),
beat spelunkers aiming for aurora,
moonwalking in chancleta hi-heel flats.
In Spanish, bat's *murciélago* (blind mouse?).
I see us all in the beer-soaked moon though:
we bump and grind, and Lupe owns the house
and Sandra swings, that reggaetón tune though . . .
so much flor y canto in our mundo
because there's no teoría without caos.

El Gúgol says they're "Mexican free-tailed,"
the bats that "migrate" to that Congress bridge
not called my back but someone's privilege
(think Congress and the suits they've never failed
and the corporate corpses they've retailed).
Electorally they'll speak "our" language:
"Yo hoblow oon pokitow." (Not a smidge.)
But who are the deported and surveilled?
Who owns our urban archipelagos?
Words privatized. Once the escuela goes,
nostalgia factories hard-sell agos
like Big Macs at the maquiladora,
but no one bats down us murciélagos!
We swarm vanilla streets till Gomorrah.

BATCODA

Running out of rhymes ending in -ora
and going batty from a lack of bats,
I map the spirit's wordless habitats,
free riffing, like Williams on his kora
(son of a fierce Boricua señora
as am I, one of many Rican brats
all born too late to be bugalú cats,
watch Clemente bat or Julia score a
run-on line.) My broomstick bat will shatter
(that Klemente rode a wooden stallion).
I'll invoke the island's antimatter,
the hemisphere's popular battalion
that claims its peace, beautiful rebellion
of bat-shit particles born to scatter.

CINQUAINS IN TRANSIT

There are   islands, and there   are mainlands, and of course   there are homelands
lost and found in   language,

sometimes   off course, others   in transit, maybe lost   to memory and found by
chance,   loose change

on the   back of a bus   or that memory in   the back of your mind, of boarding
late and

finding   a seat next to   someone who doesn't speak   your dark tongues or know
your homelands   or know

the course   but was also   born in transit, and soon   figuring out you both live in
terri-

torios   you can't translate,   on mainlands whose contours   you can't trace, so you
turn toward   the smudged

window   and you peer out   the bus as if seeking   the mainline, the headline in the
skyline,

then you   start writing down   a poem like this one,   with no lines, only the hum
of   air through

the lungs,   through these islands,   lands of is, all of which   is to say a dark song of
waves   crashing

into   you, your inlet,   your inbox, your insides,   the storm you carry with you to
the light.

STATES OF DISASSEMBLY

[SIN SEMBLANZA]

I among many   in the deafening overpass
it's demolition time   the doable, forgoable self

Y LOS CALABOZOS

I occupy   this ambit, this annex
the amber of sunset   the clunkier remix

DE MIS OJOS BORROSOS

my body as is   like a bus never full
sad or sidewinding   a function of exhaust

CAVADORA DE FOSOS

through hoists and cranes   and my eyes a semblance
of premoistened ocean   no wells around

SOCAVADORA DE GNOSIS

this walled machinery   of hate to invoice
of sickness to spreadsheet   signal lights into the ozone

GRABADORA DE VOCES

no remedies to post   no theories to posit
houses unnumbered   the welt of nations

EN EL TERRENO SIEMPRE AJENO

parked in alleys   no thru route before me
and longtime after   the swipes of empire

DEL YO Y SUS DESGLOSES

I'm too old to be carded   in these cordoned-off territories
mine is the skin's tether   too loose-tongued to linger

HACIENDO LAS PACES CON EL DETERIORO

in an atmosphere of harrows
on the outs of the moment

my history of landings
missed screenings

DE LA CIUDAD Y EL SIGNO

I clamber the ember
lowballs the remainder

the numbest of numbers
of touch on the flesh

CUANDO APENAS SE EXISTE

no skylights to open
when the body was born

no searchlights to warn
I for one was burning

A FUERZA DE CHISTE

foreclosing the tremors
I asked to be coursing

no view of the river
the hemisphere's causeways

AFUERA DE LO VIRAL

instead doubly stranded
I crash the contingent

as fuselage fragments
as mute and as mutinous

DE LA SUCURSAL DE LA IMAGEN

as a castaway blogger
on old motifs like

ghostwriting new entries
you know, the lyric self and stuff

ENTRE FLAGELACIONES COTIDIANAS

it's hard to buy this lyre
when it falls it makes a thud

nobody wants it when it's free
that sound is us

Y CANCIONES DESEANTES

confessional/confectional gimmicks
the self's presentation

jimmied locks of text
in congresses and roundtables

ABRIENDO EL FRASCO QUE DICE "RENAZCO"

lugging laptops to dive bars
for where there are widgets

in search of interconnectivity
the self is legible

Y LANZÁNDOLO HACIA EL MAR

whether the analog folds
on the digits appended

or holds all depends
to the hands interlocking

DESDE EXTRAMUROS SIN CIUDADES

in theaters and beachfronts
and will never go

where I've never been to
because going is finally a no-go

CAUTIVO DE LA HUIDA PROMETIDA

meaning's where I am
collage of bricks

this litter as is
ah, the sandlots of this land

Y ES QUE CUANDO NACEN LAS NACIONES

it's hard to play these days alone
the fires that transpired

besides I'm running out of days
did not spare these latitudes

ES DE CABEZA Y DE TERROR

and somehow the injuries
a particle's teachable moment

must become an example
if it could do more than shimmer

COMO UN ACERTIJO ESCRITO EN EL TAJO

can the shimmer be taught, shared?
in this promised land of voice where

is there co-presence
we read with silencers in hand?

EN EL BRAZO MECÁNICO DE LOS PARQUES URBANOS

must we disband
a new sense of urgency

the shock troupe that called for
embedded in this loss?

QUE SE LLENARON DE AGUANIEVE Y BALAZOS

how to wear the despair
lacking a larger scheme?

like an emblem we've made ours
all I can do is lobby for your touch

Y HAY CUERPOS MARCHANDO Y MANCHANDO ACERAS

pretending the outside
and serve up this stridency

hasn't always looked like this
that flows up the windpipe, this air

Y HAY DEVOCIONES QUE SON TAMBIÉN HORAS DURAS

my state is uncharted

and I'm ready to face the dying day traders

unlocking the shudder

becoming the ungovernable shadow

O SEA QUE DESENSAMBLEMOS EL SEMBLANTE

the ether's theremin

there, I'm in

CINQUAINS FROM TEXTS NEVER SENT

Because   fathers die and   pages fade or maybe   because islands are
bought, erased   from maps,

or else   mislabeled as   mud, as dreams of the dead,   I document
holding patterns,   standing

water,   lapsed wakefulness.   Conquistadores renamed   these shores in
their mirror image,   murdered,

enslaved,   made us namesakes,   and I am both of them,   namer and
named, as Williams knew.   From the

faucets   of capital,   mindless, mercenary   death thoughts drip
continuously.   How much?

For free.   You'll pay later,   some other way perhaps,   maybe with the
language of your   elders.

Faceless,   smiling cyborg,   I disaggregate truths.   There is an
amalgamation   (you know

just what   I mean by that),   a compound that contains   my
sedimented sentiments.   Nations

won't save   any of us,   and I am disabused   of hope, disrobed in the
landing   where they

await: execution   crews with silencer apps,   firing squads with killer
hashtags.   (My fave?

Surely   the text that kills.   Its hashtag: #killerflow.   The toxins in my
                sentences.   Talking

disease.)   Each one of us   is either a ploy or   else a duplicity machine
                always

shutting   itself off, like   a language laced with lost   lists of lusts lest it
                be loosened   at last.

IN PRAISE OF NEVERENDO

for Rev. Pedro Pietri (1943–2004)

— N —

Now the sunlit streets look comically pure as the cab creeps down Riverside Drive en route to El Barrio — and as the town car glides through Morningside I'm mourning front and center for the frowns of these forgotten statues — peering out to boundless palisades and back to the environs of Columbia — where Lorca once taught while writing *Poeta en Nueva York* — so close yet so far from your Harlem of "bulletproof rice and beans"

— E —

Even though I want to cry I let the cabdriver complain about insurance and the price of gas — he says cab fare will go up like the middle finger of the grocery-grabbing grandma he just nearly ran over — **olvídate, que ahora se puso fea la cosa y está mala la ciudad** — and the town car tumbles toward Lexington Avenue

— V —

Vaya — sometimes I think this city is too much for me and I'm too much in tune with muted elsewheres — sometimes I grow tired of living up to domestic Boricua prerequisites of living as bored equals under the traumatic neon of reggaetón and poetry slams — **a veces necesito la apertura de ventanas innecesarias** — of impossible bookshelves — **para desmontar y equilibrar ensueños** — and those are the times when I pick up Pietri's "Prologue for Ode to Road Runner" and trade in the town car to ride the mind shotgun on "A downtown train / A train downtown / train A town down / down A train town"

— E —

Each one of us in this city where no promise is preserved rides on with rearview visions that cannot be reduced to mass market chronology — all we have is the promise of the poet recast as lifelines outside the confines of sound byte space-time

Reverendo Neverendo — I promise to read you facing the front lines — defacing the headlines — reading as best I can through the worry lines of faces — to the lines of the faithful huddled outside these lion-less libraries — where your thunder's being called for by the wind — has not yet reached but so soon will — voiding all passports to institute a new enterprise of freedom

Elegy means I vow to use your words to disarm the power nap conspirators — to not replay the corporate charades of fake art exhibit angst — to burn down the mind rot cubicle compartments — to furnish these imaginary apartments with your bile and bravura — I vow to learn to sing in lapsed hangover slang and translate "La cuna blanca" into your black truth serum

Nadie se atreva a llorar — dejen que ría no en silencio — sino en overjoyous y epiphanic tongues — your loose joint certitude — language unhinged for all to see — and to claim citizenship in your roadrunner republic of punk **coyotismo**

Demos gracias to the storied Neverendo — the original distributor of democratic poison doses — the undertaker of the overseeing of post–**ceguera ciudadanos** — the urban nightmare's outfitter of hope — the one who dared us to depose the monuments of nations and remake them in our name

Okay — so let's sing from the unspoiled beaches of remembering — from the bottomless pulpit of these walkup high-rises — where we carry on your role as sleepless strategists — with embraces emblazoned and rhymes underway — calling out the names of Neverendo from the urgent soil of our cities

NOBODY'S HOME

upstate cinquains

Now watch / me as I trip, / tripartite: bloody, buzzed, / rootless in the age of routers, / rooting // for sun / in the gray snow, / palms in frozen cities, / looking back and missing the road / before // my eyes, / eroding this / expanse. Can homelands stand / or just fizzle into mindscape, / now that // mothers / live alone and / lean on the verandas / of endless summers? Nostalgia / kills us. // Resist / the passing of / time measured in '80s / soul collections. So where is / our / birthright, // I mean, / our connection / to skin? What do we have / but pop-culture flotsam, sampling / ring tones // and beats? / Perhaps the skin / is all in the synapse, / the rest is skeleton scansion. / Perhaps // my drive / is very low / on memory, with the / coatracks and 8-tracks of childhood / now filed // away / under "missing." / But I'm on the way back / to the beachfront towns that birthed us, / you know, // the ones / with Pizza Huts / and zinc roofs side by side? / Besideness is the only way. / There's no // soundtrack / b-sides. No fries / with that. No more bio. / Biological families / deposed. // Angles / of sunlight now / must stand for belonging, / since islands are blurred, cities gassed, / all meals // to go, / poets goateed, / blogging at the ether / net cables of oblivion. / Today // we are / other than wise, / otherwise occupied / with staving off the loneliness / of our // living / in corporate / bones, with no past except / as injury. Where is home now? / Home is // what you / can't flip. No switch. / No script. No beach condo. / You come up with some platitudes / cribbed from // postcards. / Dust boulevards. / Governors' mansions with / mango trees and manicured yards / turning // to shards. / Come up to breathe. / Come up to breathe for once. / Turn to neighbors and ask yourself / "what now?" // This is / not my island, / and I am no man yet. / Still a child. Don't call me out for / failing // to see, / to remember. / Please. I'll call you instead. / We'll talk about what to forget / next or, // better, / what to forgo. / Foreground rhythm when you can. / If you forget faces maybe / words will // lead you / back home again. / Forget the scenery. / Unseen are the truer senses. / Meaning's // fences. / Truth not pictured. / And so this road leads where? / Write this one down, faux Baudelaire: / no one // home now, / correspondence / can only be picked up / far away from home. Letters sent / elsewhere. // Language / is like a mesh / of our own making. Still / waking up. We're trees after the / tremors.

UNSTATEMENTS   (UPSTATE SKY)

talking poem   *voice notes*   *State Street*   *Albany*

"And I will make a song of the organic bargains of These States"

—WALT WHITMAN

12:34 pm   the state building before me   whose?   construction sites   interference of spring   angle of wires   stateless   but not wireless yet

12:35   over the brownstones   the nice nineteenth-century colonials   (me, I'm twenty-first)   it towers   (why so?)   the state building   the late '60s columns   the tint and the glass   the boxy presence

12:36   I tried to feel utilitarian once   in the presence of those buildings worked there   organized   cubicled   lit fluorescent   in early afternoons   Post-its and memos?   no memo now

12:37   now memory is speak-only   at last   (keep your ROM)   the mystery of memory   in cities   well. it's shared   not well but still   the difficulty that defines the song and its trappings   the sky

12:39   I've turned left   the state building now behind me   now potted planters overturned   incipience of leaves   plastic chairs   flowers   an impromptu garden

12:41   let me say more   there are no fire escapes here   just ladders   steps white siding   against the off-white sky   somehow today blue   rust on brick   a blinding combination   and yes I'm still   in a construction site

12:42   I've turned right from the state building   a tangle of branches again are those Budweiser bottles   next to the beach chairs   on the deck next door   still dim?   maybe a Michelob   maybe a stutter step?

12:43   far above   a second state building   no!   wait!   the real one!   the site of protests   in budget shortfall   free fall days like these   I never noticed   modernist stone   and those arches   Gothic perhaps?

12:45   there's an archness to the culture   to these times   it makes sense somehow   that before me   hammock   picket fence   Volvo   and a tattered American flag   fight it out for prominence   between the tangle of branches

12:47   the point is that speaking   is always an absence   and speaking of absence I am the self's speaking   bad stance   before an open sky   always interference   in this case   an antenna

12:50   again everything around me   is wires and noise   what happened to the wireless morning?   the discreet hum?   the promised copresence?   I told you about the mic'd breezeway   well here it is again

12:51   how could you write   a poem of these states?   as interference maybe this stasis   yes there is a wreath   laurel muted   on a neighbor's window   the basement door in need of paint   yes there are neighbors

12:52   yes there is blood   in this expanse   a beat   but does it know no interference?   what can it know   as blue tarp and blue sky   bleed into one?

12:54   mine   is the constriction site   of speaking   that's my expanse   take it   leave it   that's all that's left   to mine   a plastic bag   tangled in the branches

12:55   it makes its own   kind of   music   can you hear it?   faint rustle those aren't berries   those planters cannot hold   and still   the cities hold   the holed-up neighbors

12:56   they slowly emerge   for this is spring   after all   in their step   is that graffiti   in the distance   by the nineteenth-century brick?   more interference   ugly green   early '70s siding   siting   sighting   citing

12:57   we're so aware of temporality   or at least I am   we have a decade for everything   and it goes double for centuries   always doubled   our temp   orality the medium and   the mess . . .

1:00   I'm not sure   what the terms mean anymore   the welcome mats are dirty   whose citizens?   I wasn't born here   but then again I was   stateless remember?   so many of us were

60

1:01   this thing about belonging   maybe back to text   print as belonging

1:02   maybe my voice here   is boutique   nothing as lonely as openness only expanse

1:06   besides   closed and open meet   between the voice   and its technologies the freeform   and its framing   all art is framing

1:07   even when it frames itself   or the city   as in graffiti   or frames the audience   as in Duchamp   I'm sitting down now

1:08   I'm tired of dispensing   I'll speak the city as tonal shifts   SO THINK OF THIS AS BLOCK CAPITALS   the capital's blocks aren't always ugly

1:09   the street is still the "I"   and its opening   call it the spleen   of Albany nothing's opening   state workers   probably out to lunch by now   people clerking networking   some lurking

1:11   everything's off   except the BlackBerries   at the Italian restaurants   by the courthouse

1:12   interconnectivity   stops for no one   but I must stop   so if you're hedging your bets   on America's Next   I can't help you   few hedges here   more wires

1:13   what would happen   if I scaled a rooftop   and snipped a wire or two set fire to the connective tissue?   likely not too much   a bit more interference?   they'd make do

1:15   let's get metaphysical   let me hear your   wireless anima talk   maybe have a conversation   chat without   the chattel

1:17   I'm not sure what that means   it means that clouds   are peeking over the state building

1:20   I'm a function of thrift stores   and minor symbolists   so what is my status update?   stateless but reinstated?   recovering the spring of America   the mechanical noise   it's all I know

THE COLONIAL ZONE

Santo Domingo cinquains

D. R.   Aurora reads   the wrinkles of my palms   like signs in the colonial   city.

She tells   me all about   a cruisy corner bar   where guys in too-tight tees and jeans
drink and

show off   perishable   goods (I can almost see   an impetuous angel drown   in
seas

of skin   while up onstage   the brown-eyed drag queen works   the packed room
with little more than   her mic,

her laugh   ten times the size   of her shoes). Aurora   hands me an unreadable map
and leaves,

smiling.   I start to walk   faster and faster past   ladies carrying shopping bags,
huffing

uphill,   their baseball-capped   husbands and sons behind   them, counting the
footsteps to the   next store.

I turn   right and follow   the old city's contours,   seeking out panoramic views
that will

connect   present and past: an empire's ruins and   its restless stepchildren, of
which   I too

am one,   prodigally.   A man sells necklaces,   sees me walking by and mumbles
something

backed by   the cool trade winds,   but the rumbling of trucks   sounds like a
tractatus on the   import-

export   logic of the   neoliberal age.   Emerging at last from the zone's   tangled

bodies,   I ask out loud   who owns el Caribe   as I make my way across an   empty

parking   lot, palms in my   pockets and nobody   around, alone, remembering
embers

of dreams,   cleansed spirit haunts,   Aurora, blood of palms   in the blooming
graveyards of our   ocean.

BRONX CROWN

at the late Crown Donut diner, the Bronx, 2010, after Marilyn Hacker and Patricia Smith

I pledge allegiance to the stateless crew.
The night's estate. Lampposts over gravel.
Bodies that make do and makes that travel
Past vacant lots onto the avenue
Unearthing the internal revenue
You don't declare: a mess of hardscrabble
Skin, songs, in-jokes, lovers' names to babble,
Remixed melodies, and memories to
Drum. All the stuff too tough for you to hum,
It comes back in a feedback loop of pain
Meant for release. City continuum
We live for. Who says Wonder sings in vain?
And like a DJ with an amped-up plate
I pledge allegiance to the night's estate.

I pledge allegiance to the night's estate
In crude syllabics. An all-night diner
With no sign, no special. In a minor
Key, some ring tone moans. A hot late-night date?
Sounds measured in those smiles commensurate
With sex. You say, "Baby, no one's finer!"
And crank up Marvin. You're alone. Wine or
Wi-Fi are your companions. "Life is great!"
You say. It is. At least till you look up
And the wine's gone. Now Lady Gaga wails.
You're wireless and yet in need of hookups
(Men, women, both). You and your fairy tails!
The night's estate finds you whole, ecstatic
(Perhaps the phrasing's a bit dramatic).

Perhaps the phrasing's a bit dramatic,
Such are the trappings of a sonnet crown.
(Take note: *not* the Coronas you gulped down,
The squirt of lime, arch and programmatic,
Last night karaokeing through static
On oldies night: "Take me to . . . Funkytown!"
"P-push it real good!" "James Brown! James Brown!"
"White lines!" "Automatic, systematic . . ."
"Let the music play . . ." "One mic . . ." "Boogie nights . . ."
"You come and go . . ." "I live by the river!")
Your iPod shuffles. Yankee Stadium's lights
Drown the muted moon as scalpers shiver,
Trumped up gold embalms the subway station.
Evil empires call for coronation.

Evil empires call for coronation,
Forgetting the nation is a chorus,
Its boundaries beautifully porous,
And we're the skin, song's reverberation,
Black, brown, red, and yellow. We're the nation
That topples the dying Mediasaurus
Whose cameras typecast or ignore us;
We don't need their wack representations
(Gold crowns? Crown Fried Chicken? Try Crotona
Park on Sundays. Not quite Corona, Queens,
Or Crown Heights. *Bronx* crown!). My Smith Corona's
Handheld, and still I scat my crowning scenes,
My voice at once resplendent and rundown.
A crown of thorns is still a bloody crown.

A crown of thorns is still a bloody crown,
And crowns are subject to their colonies.
The migrant city and its litanies
Frame our epic, feed the plural pronoun,
Drown out nativist statesmen (is that *Drown*
As in Junot or as in mermaid seas
Full of those guardian angel manatees

Whose big lips point to safety, giant gowns
Of sound in sine-wave sonero tropics?).
Our ancestors survived by telling jokes
About conquest, on point or off topic,
And now we call out Wall Street for its hoax.
No cities of gold, Don Coronado,
Home is where the skyline meets the shadow.

Home is where the skyline meets the shadow.
Where's P. R.? (Orlando? Pennsylvania?)
Our common wealth of heart and crania
(The "us" that still matters). El Dorado
Looks like sunset on the Concourse: Auto
Parts. Vivero beats of Morissania.
Hips that swivel. Drums. Rum. Chill mania
Of block parties. Abuelas' bliss blotto.
Old club queens munch on love's stale granola
While salsa boy heartbreak hugs the distance.
Mine is no royal crown, just flat cola.
Crows have flown. My flow meets its resistance.
Crown me, Bronx streets, with your uneasy swing.
I'll write a crown where everyone is king.

I'll write a crown where everyone is king
And let the royal flushes abdicate;
They'll fall away or fall for a fool's mate,
Or else they'll simply fall (a funny thing,
Just watch, you wait). They'll get their reckoning,
And we at last will get to voice our fate.
To pledge allegiance to the night's estate
Means for once remembering how to sing
The song with no words, the old primal hum
Of spirits from the heat of sugarcane
And coffee hills. Is this delirium
Or tedium? Will we transcend our pain?
The pain that made us also made our chant.
Our skin remembers what our language can't.

Our skin remembers what our language can't
Like ashes from a fire that never was
Except as embers in the mind's eye. Does
It seem odd that when the right words are scant
I make them up, I mumble, or I rant
Or let the syllables just work their buzz
And overwhelm my neurons just because?
What if a poet is a sycophant
Of form and no one buys her flattery?
And what if Whitman's stately spoken word
Were remixed on phones low on battery?
How would that sound: predestined or absurd?
Who says we have to sample *Leaves of Grass*?
We're ghosts of poets by the overpass.

We're ghosts of poets by the overpass.
Desiring beats, the DJ's roughest trade,
Our rhymes are fresh and somehow retrograde,
Born daydreaming in remedial class,
Wishing, hoping that we would somehow pass
And passing notes and grubbing, not for grades,
But for a deeper sense of that which made
Us who we were: at once shy and wiseass
Children of the impasse, when our dark eyes
Betrayed us as we scribbled with no end
Except to somehow dematerialize
Into the city's ether, ballpoint penned.
Even then, we were stateless, it was clear,
Still haunted by the ships that brought us here.

Still haunted by the ships that brought us here
Where ecocide and Middle Passage meet,
A movement that's as obvious as the street
(And as hard). Spaceships in the atmosphere
Can't match our moves, the queer ways that we steer
Through traffic jams while huffing the concrete
To catch the express bus without a seat.

The driver sighs and stares past the mirror.
He sees the sun's veneer over the gray
Of fire escapes. América's city,
Who wrote you and what does your first tag say?
Let me trace your source: fresh, sooty, pretty.
I wasn't born here, only born again.
I'm singing out of state y tú también.

I'm singing out of state y tú también.
I'm new jack, yes, and wannabe, perhaps.
I learned from books (Mohr's *El Bronx*, Cruz's *Snaps*)
And each Diasporican denizen
Who dares spit rhymes. My uptown Borikén
Cannot be mapped with visual aids or apps,
I learned it first by ear, then by synapse
And slowly I applied it to the pen.
My beat is fair, my rhymes ordinary
Compared to those who walked here long before
(KRS-One, Barretto, Palmieri
Or the old lady going to the store).
The sun slants over clotheslines as I wake.
Here is the litany I just can't shake.

Here is the litany I just can't shake
Because it's written like a molten glyph
Into the flesh of each networking stiff
That calls you home, not knowing what she'll make
Or how they'll pay the rent. Now, an outtake
From my film: a drag queen lights up a spliff,
Inhales slowly, and asks herself, "what if?"
An ice-cream truck goes by. The end. Remake?
OK, instead she asks herself, "why me?" . . .
In each case the film stock would be sepia
And the whole thing would be made for TV.
Don't wanna hear it? Don't let me keep ya.
I'll stay with the film reel inside my head
Till you finally wake me from the dead.

Till you finally wake me from the dead
I'll write obituaries (Pietri did)
Above all for the living, hopes that hid
Still living on the streets and in my head.
Will you please put some luz in my loose thread
So I can then transition off the grid
Of mainland? Become island in eyelid,
An inner landscape better left unsaid
Except as a punchline with no setup
That leaves them rolling in the tropic isles
Where severed heads are more than death's getup;
Just ask the sharks patrolling all these miles.
The spirit home we build is what matters.
The body grows and grays till it scatters.

The body grows and grays till it scatters.
The city booms, then gentrifies, then busts.
The subway runs and stops, and then it rusts.
The nation-state holds on till it shatters.
The self in doubt, the homelands in tatters.
The politics of buyout and mistrust.
The knobs and tuners that we can't adjust.
The particle of voice antimatters.
The dry-dock of a ship with no rudder.
The close-up of planets with no tether.
The love and shame empty in a shudder.
The mass of us, one mess all together.
We're out of state but coming into view.
I pledge allegiance to the stateless crew.

I pledge allegiance to the night's estate
(Perhaps the phrasing's a bit dramatic).
Evil empires call for coronation.
A crown of thorns is still a bloody crown.
Home is where the skyline meets the shadow.
I'll write a crown where everyone is king.
Our skin remembers what our language can't.

We're ghosts of poets by the overpass
Still haunted by the ships that brought us here.
I'm singing out of state y tú también.
Here is the litany I just can't shake
Till you finally wake me from the dead.
The body grows and grays till it scatters.
I pledge allegiance to the stateless crew.

POSTSCRYPT

under lockdown, the Bronx, 2020

When capitalism is a virus
That's knocking on each barricaded door,
We summon all the dead from the long war
To weaponize, silence, and hellfire us.
Corona? Our bodies crowned, desirous,
A furious light too brilliant to ignore.
We won't let them erase us anymore.
Our skin, a stateless scroll, dream papyrus
That maps hidden shores in rhymed polemic.
We heed the Earth and let it legislate.
Capital becomes its own pandemic.
We pledge allegiance to the night's estate,
The dark seed in us, fractal residue.
We pledge allegiance to the flagless crew.

FOUND ANTHEM

for Puerto Rico

Mental void, panacea, aporia,
hurricane, network of smoke:

live, don't be the neoliberal atlas,
words on the bus of worlds.

Don't improvise faces,
trace dungeons in the always alien land

of the city and the sign,
captive to a promised flight.

In other words, let's disassemble the visage
of the conquistadores who piss on us

so as to balance daydreams,
fiercely, not in silence.

Nostalgia doesn't live in us.
The hound eats, strong and resilient.

With axes and machetes we escape,
mining the capital in our tones.

The rich are over, done with. You'll be the saga, the sound
of Lorca's car in wastelands with nameless owners.

Stay, stay, be the net, the salsa singer
whose golden voice sums up death

and also escapes, inhaling sepia light.
We are millions, and so are you.

Mental nada panacea aporía huracán hum o red palabras mundo bus no improvise faces trace
calabozos en el terreno siempre ajeno de la ciudad y el signo cautivo de la huida prometida o sea que
desensamblemos el semblante conquistadores mean para desmontar y equilibrar ensueños bravura no
en silencio nostALGia no more come can fuerte fuerte hacha y machete escapes mine tonal capital more
se acabaron los ricos sea saga Lorca sonAR auto estos páramos con dueños anónimos red estate estate
soneros el dorado mate concrete escapes también INhales sepia luz miles y tú también.

MARES DISPARES
DISPARATE SEAS

he aquí todo lo que cabe
entre el mar caribe y el atlántico norte.
he aquí: mi imaginario.

here i have all that fits
between the caribbean sea and the north atlantic.
here i have: my imaginary.

—RAQUEL SALAS RIVERA, *LO TERCIARIO / THE TERTIARY*

ECO COLONIAL

ESPEJISMOS

cierta claridad que falta
ciudad esmaltada
gris animación silente

fuiste un torbellino estelar
y ahora habitas
un cuarto sin luz

hay voces ansiosas
allanando tu cabeza
que es la mía salvo que

sin postes de luz
se pierde la huella
de lo que siempre vemos

busco el ojo interno
donde muelen los vidrios
de una historia sangrienta

COLONIAL ECHO

MIRAGES

a certain missing clarity
glazed city
silent gray animation

you were a stellar storm
and now you inhabit
a windowless room

unsettled voices
overtake your head
which is mine except that

without lampposts
they can't follow the trace
of what we always see

i'm after that inner eye
where they grind the glass
for a history of blood

DESPLEGARIA

vértebras de islas
que crujen con los años

vertedero de nuestros ojos
ventriloquía de arena

playas de metralla
ciudadanía de tormenteras

mares termoplásticos
traspasan la red del sueño

la granulosidad de la voz
ampolla solar

desde amplitudes mínimas
retomemos cuentas

el eco colonial muere
en nuestro canto en llamas

UNSUPPLICATION

the spines of islands
creaking with years

landfill of our eyes
ventriloquy of sand

beaches made of shrapnel
storm-shutter citizenship

thermoplastic seas
piercing the net of dreams

granular voice
sunstruck and blistering

from minimal amplitudes
let's reclaim the tallies

the colonial echo dies
in the flames of our song

PSALM (44 PALAVERS)
ODIA (44 PALABRAS)

*"You have given us up like sheep intended for food,
And have scattered us among the nations."*

—PSALM 44

nombra tu primer año asesino en la ciudad ausente del antropoceno y la falsa
name if you can your first murderous year in this city of anthropocene
absences and remember the conversations you had with no face just a dollop
of sky and a brutal assault of retail spite and rhymes to remind you of what's
after air

modestia del plancton en las cuevas galácticas o pueblo de ardides frente a la
who will hear the humblebrag of plankton in the coves of galaxies as pretty
and far as the kiss never given and how much howling from those other
possible worlds will seep through the plastic motherboard so the goddesses
can catch us clicking ash?

frontera nevada donde nos buscamos como quien da mamadas y traga apenas
there is a town of ruses near the snowy border where we seek each other out
and yet guttural logic fails and sidewinder music gives way to surveilled napes
and eyes of gristle and there is no net at the bottom of the sea

su propia flema y se da cuenta que las políticas del cuerpo a nadie salvan
when you give head and swallow only your own phlegm is when you realize
body politics won't save you even though there's no other kind so your savior
is the dank smell you savor in the taint as tanks and bloody punchlines empty
streets

aunque hay abuelas en la última galaxia esperándonos para darnos cama y
sopa

> there are grandmothers in the last galaxy waiting to take us in and heal our
> skin and syncretize souls in soup and remind us that we are our accidents
> and accents finding freedom in the brackish water with no silencers on our
> misremembered joy

y sanarnos sincretizando almas de cuatro mil muertos cuarenticuatro calibres

> four thousand deaths mean eight thousand shoes and forty-four caliber
> palavers without pallbearers because cadavers sing the psalm of respite under
> chemical skies where estuary water meets the sea by our toes that stubbornly
> claim these islands of dreams and drums where every revolution is unhomely

sin pesebres libres islas soñadas donde toda revolución es apátrida

CARIBES

anagrammatic song

canto anagramático

escriba		re basic
	caribes	
bisecar		rice abs
	caribes	
escibar		bi races
	caribes	
caribes		scab ire
	criba es	
si caber		i braces
	caribes	
recibas		bars ice
	caribes	
si cebar		bi scare
	caribes	
caribes		bear [sic]
	brea [sic]	
ciberas		bias rec
	caribes	
brisca 'e		brie sac
	caribes	
creas bi-		sib acre
	caribes	
caribes		rib case
	césar bi	

si cebra   bise arc

     caribes

si becar   sib care

     caribes

si cabré   ace ribs

     caribes

caribes   cri base

     ¡sí cabré!

brisa ce   i.e., carbs

     caribes

casi ber   i.e., crabs

     caribes

bárices   abc rise

     caribes

caribes   arcs i be

     crea [bis]

ascribe   caribes

a scribe   caribes

sea crib   caribes

caribes   i be scar

ijla kontinente   aksilaj i kueroj   kueroj i aksilaj   anunsioj de deteljente   fantajmaj
mochileroj   ke peldieron suj mochilaj   dokumentando suj biajej   pol la américa
nuejtra   komo selajej de otra   ijkielda siniejtra   ke suplanta y sekuejtra   a la
anteriol   i otro gobielno en flol   se malchita   i otro potro de derecha   kabesea
i se enkabrita   asumiendo la mueka maltrecha   de laj masaj de ejtrasa   i ai filaj
en todoj loj beltederoj   bajo el sol de la mañana   i ya se siente ke van dejpeltando
i de kuando en kuando   se abre una bentana   i ej ke akí   si bien no me ekiboko
todo sana   poko a poko   lentamente

FONETIKANTO

áilan' kóntinen'   néiked lands   néiked kousts   ditéryen' brands   bákpaker
gousts   ju lost der bákpaks   dókumentin' der bóyech   akrós aur américa   laik
kláudskeips of anódel   lef'-bijáin' lef'   dat suplants an jáiyaks   de príbius uan
an' anódel góbelmen' in blum   uíders auei   an' anódel ráituing koult   chímis and
chéiks   uéring de báterd grímes   of de braun-péiper máses   an' der ar lon' lains
in ol de dómpin' graunds   óndel de mólnin' son   an' uan kan fil dem auéikenin'
an' ébri uans in a uail   a uíndou óupens   an' so yu si   ébrisin biguins tu jíal
bit bai bit   ibéntuali

HUMBOLDTIANDO

improvisación   *videovocal*   improvisation   Humboldt Park   Chicago

in Humboldt Park I'm humbled   I wander through the streets   and want my
handheld   to communicate my hunger
        en Humboldt Park   ombligo de mi parca voz   me vuelvo por las calles
y quiero que mi inalámbrico   comunique mi hambre

this city   isn't hobbled   a hub of skin here   a smile   a scar   inhabited
        esta ciudad   no cojea   hay un núcleo de piel aquí   una sonrisa
una cicatriz   habitada

heaven is here   past Yauco Food and Liquors   past the flags and tags
        el edén está aquí   pasando Yauco Food and Liquors   pasando las
banderas y el grafiti

this time I'm Albizu's visitor   making smokestack sounds   in cities without
soundtrack
        esta vez visito a Albizu   haciendo ruidos de chimenea de otrora   en
ciudades sin banda sonora

to be here   is to amble   to mumble   fading sun   graying sky
        estar aquí   es deambular   es farfullar   el sol desdibujándonos   el
cielo gris

rhymes   battle-scarred   in bateyes   passing Jayuya Barber Shop   and Adalberto's
United Methodist Church   and Cardenal's Driving School
        rimas   cicatrices de guerras   en bateyes   pasando Jayuya Barber
Shop   y Adalberto's United Methodist Church   y Cardenal's Driving School

the only drive here   is the urgency of history   not yet seeping   through the noise
of a late-winter afternoon
        lo que me conduce aquí   es la urgencia de la historia   que aún no se
filtra   entre el ruido   de una tarde de fines de invierno

they say recidivism   is a social responsibility   they say *farmacia* and *café cola'o*   they
say *oficina de equipo médico*   but what are we equipped for really?

       dicen que la reincidencia   es un deber social   dicen *farmacia y café
cola'o*   dicen *oficina de equipo médico*   pero ¿para qué estamos equipados?
¿a qué equipo le vamos?

¿a qué equipo le vamos?   ya no equiparables a una isla   un archipiélago
una piel   un Lago Michigan   entre ojo y ojo

       what team do we root for?   no longer comparable to an island   an
archipelago   a skin   a Lake Michigan   between the eyes

no parking dicen   en la ciudad vacía   pues no estaciono   dame mejor
las estaciones múltiples   del éxtasis

       they say no parking   in the empty city   so I don't park   give me instead
the many seasons   of ecstasy

no pasan taxis   mas pasan mis rimas   por los supermercados   las
fruterías   el Luquillo Barbershop   el dios que hace delivery   por calles
como estas   calles que restan   pero que suman a algo

       no taxis going by   only my rhymes   along the supermarkets   the fruit
stands   the Luquillo Barbershop   the god that delivers   down streets like these
left over   but adding up to something

¿y este caminar?   ¿cómo contrarrestarlo?   ¿cómo contraponer   el calor de
una voz   al frío maquinal?

       and this walking   how to counteract it?   how to contrast   a voice's warmth
with the mechanical cold?

tengo moquillo   tengo ansia de botánica   tengo la gana anímica   de andar
de parrandear por otras calles   como estas

       I have the sniffles   I'm jonesing for some botánica herbs in my verbs   and
I'd be up   for ambling   for carousing   through some other streets like these

no puede ser   que Albizu y Muñoz Marín   coexistan en estas calles   juntos
y encallados   como las rimas   de estos minutos   callados   pero hallados
al lado   de otro cuerpo   como el de uno . . .   (no hay ninguno)   como el
de uno . . .   (no hay ninguno)   calles ninguneadas   lo son todo   si bien
no hay ningún hada

it can't be   Pedro Albizu Campos and Luis Muñoz Marín   coexisting on
these streets   run aground together   like the rhymes   that frame these quiet times
when you walk in stride alongside   another body   like your own . . .   (there
is none)   like your own . . .   (there is none)   scorned streets that sing   are
everything   no need for fairy tales

olvidemos la nostalgia   este Chicago   no es el chic   del long ago   la re-
memoria fácil   me queda chiquita   pero me quedo aquí   quieto   rimando
en combustión   "espontánica" de botánica   entre tanta emergencia   hay
una efervescencia   . . . esencia

      let's forget the nostalgia   this Chicago   ain't the chic   from long ago   the
easy reminiscence   doesn't fit me anymore   but I'm still here   chill   rhyming in
"spontanic"   botánica combustion   and for all my convalescence   there's still an
effervescence   . . . an essence

no es ciencia esto   lo bien que coexistimos   Guerrero's Tacos and Pizza
al lado de Iglesia de Dios Peniel   gracias pastora América Yolanda García
gracias Supermercado Municipal   gracias El Quijote Artesanía de Puerto Rico
gracias People's Choice Mortgage Corp.   por habitar estas calles   por evitar
que yo calle

      this ain't no science   how well we coexist   Guerrero's Tacos and Pizza
next to Iglesia de Dios Peniel   thank you pastora América Yolanda García   thank you
Supermercado Municipal   thank you El Quijote Artesanía de Puerto Rico   thank you
People's Choice Mortgage Corp.   for inhabiting these streets   for allowing me to
speak

esta calle se llama *Division*   ¿nombre irónico o protagónico?   no llego
a divisar   me miran raro acá   igual que en Río Piedras   igual que en
el Bronx   igual que ésta y otras   calles sin reparo   respiro al garo
algarabía   al garabato   algazara no hay   solo de voz   devoción   en vez
de división   divagación   cruzar de calles   solo   cruzar

      this street is called Division   is that name ironic or omniscient?   something
I can't envision   they look at me funny here   the same as in San Juan   the same as
in the Bronx   the same as all the other   streets without reprieve   I breathe without
a clue   a hullabaloo   of scribbles   the hubbub's   all been dubbed   devotion
instead of division   digression   streets to be crossed   just me   crossing

BAGKU

written on plastic bodega bags

escritos en bolsitas plásticas

Voz sin estado,
entona, ciudadano,
tu mar rimado.

Bagku know no state.
Citizens of baggy style,
syllable and song.

Plásticas bolsas,
¡para botar las sobras
de la poesía!

Institutional
art critique with plastic bags
is family fun.

Ciudad soñada,
sin bolsa de valores
pero con flores.

Dreams of a city
where sleeping body bags lie.
Sing, bagabond bones!

Haikú anarcos,
basuras de Bakunin,
¡qué bien desunen!

Bakunin was an
anarchist who died in Bern . . .
baby, burn bag flags!

Glifos del éter
con o sin documentos,
aire que somos.

Undocumented
art that documents airspace.
Glyphs in the ether.

P. R. AYER

La curación del cielo empieza ahora junto al remolque bajo el puente donde
duermen los rehenes que nacen en tus ojos.
> The recovery of the sky begins now by the trailer under the bridge that
> houses the hostages in your eyes.

Protestamos por lo bajo hasta que se cuece un grito entre los **vertederos de** la
voz.
> We protest under our breath until a scream seethes amid the **graveyards of**
> the voice.

Ante las luchas virtuales me veo solo y sin cimientos pero miento si te digo que
no te deseo, si te digo que me quiero.
> Locked in virtual struggles I see myself alone with no foundation yet I'd be
> lying if I said I didn't dig you, if I said I loved myself.

Esta calle siempre fue mi favorita.
> This street was always my favorite.

Tendrá que ver con la **luz** que se cuela entre nosotros o quizás con que nunca
acabamos de crecer y seguimos baladíes pero agradecidos de nuestro aliento en
los distritos del grito garabateado en cada pared.
> It must have to do with the **light** that seeps through us or with our never
> growing up and with the fact that we're still inconsequential yet grateful for our
> breath in districts where cries are scrawled on every wall.

Y como sea sobrevivimos como reptiles o proyectiles de guerras pasadas en esta
isla que **nos toca caminar**, con el peso de lo perdido.
> And somehow we survive like reptiles or projectiles from past wars on this
> island **we must walk**, with the weight of what was lost.

Somos ciudadanos de mares dispares.
> We are citizens of disparate seas.

HAY(NA)KU BORICUA

nos
toca caminar
vertederos de luz

graveyards
of light
we must walk

JULIÉCIMAS

"My cry that is no more mine,
"Inútilmente estiro
but hers and his forever [. . .]
mi camino sin luces.
the comrades of my silence,
Como muertos sin sitio
the phantoms of my grave."
se sublevan mis voces."

—JULIA DE BURGOS, "FAREWELL IN WELFARE ISLAND"
—JULIA DE BURGOS, "OH MAR, NO ESPERES MÁS"

Now poetry is just a name
Tras de la poesía
for this, our faint embodied sound,
nos queda lo sonoro
for music once it's not around,
sin palabras ni coro,
for ash in lockstep with the flame,
cuerpos en entropía.
for streets still summoning the same
La calle todavía
old shadows. Watch buses sever
pide sombras. No cruces
concrete. No, this war will never
sin ver los autobuses,
end. Yes, our breath is the front line.
la guerra que respiro.
Sing: My cry that is no more mine,
Inútilmente estiro
but hers and his forever.
mi camino sin luces.

Our war is in the wounds we brought
        La guerra que se trajo
from our archipelagic ports,
        de puertos tropicales
making us dark echoes of sorts,
        nos hizo sucursales
boneyard of songs, islands of thought
        de huesos, un refajo
shaped by blood currents under clot
        de islas en el tajo
of empire. Until Julia gave
        de imperios. Soy desgloses
us back our ghosts and dared the slave
        de Julia (¿la conoces?)
to disinter her violence.
        bajo un cielo de litio.
Sing: *the comrades of my silence,*
        Como muertos sin sitio
the phantoms of my grave.
        se sublevan mis voces.

CATORCE ASTROS

homenaje al "Soneto de la estrellas" de Esteban Valdés (presente)

```
**************
*************S
************OS
***********ROS
**********TROS
*********STROS
********ASTROS
*******EASTROS
******CEASTROS
*****RCEASTROS
****ORCEASTROS
***TORCEASTROS
**ATORCEASTROS
*CATORCEASTROS
```

FOURTEEN STARS

after "Soneto de las estrellas" by Esteban Valdés (present)

```
**************
*************S
************RS
***********ARS
**********TARS
*********STARS
********NSTARS
*******ENSTARS
******EENSTARS
*****TEENSTARS
****RTEENSTARS
***URTEENSTARS
**OURTEENSTARS
*FOURTEENSTARS
```

PERIODO ESPACIAL
SPATIAL PERIOD

cuaderna vía láctea

neobroke cuaderna vía

Hoy veo lo que eres y todo lo que fuiste.
> Now I see all you are and all you used to be.

Tus curvas sin esfuerzo. Tu cara de despiste.
> Your effortless contours daydreaming next to me.

Tu impavidez de faro. Tu oscuridad que insiste.
> Your stillness is a light. Beaming geography.

La voz hecha costuras del olvidado chiste.
> I can't recall that joke you told me constantly.

Hoy veo lo que fuiste y todo lo que eres.
> Now I see all you were and everything you are.

La forma en que desvistes el hábitat de enseres.
> How you undress the earth under desire's lodestar.

Después de la derrota de hombres y mujeres.
> I love the way your eyes uncover every scar.

En el largometraje de cines sin ujieres.
> An empty cineplex without your avatar.

Tu cara de despiste. Tus curvas sin esfuerzo
> Your effortless contours. Your lips just as they purse.

Tapizan los pasillos del último universo.
> Your shape enveloping each fallen universe.

Donde músicas mueren das luz a lo disperso
> Where music goes to die you make darkness disperse.

En vértigo de prosa y pronación de verso.
> In vertiginous prose and pronations of verse.

¿Cómo se codifica tu impavidez de faro?

       How can I codify the stillness of your light?

¿Quién correrá programas en el lenguaje raro

       Who'll execute programs in your language of flight?

De tu orbital en ruina? Tu brisa sin reparo.

       Your orbit in ruins the winds can't overwrite.

Desierto boreal de glaciar y saguaro.

       Your boreal desert of cactus and frostbite.

Estos videojuegos de la voz en costuras.

       Play the video games of the voice and its seams.

Realidad virtual o flor de amarguras.

       This virtually real flower of dark dreams.

El avatar de huesos. Las cruces que depuras.

       The avatar of bones surrenders all its schemes.

El archivo comprime las sangrientas anchuras.

       Your smile corrupts the file and its bloody regimes.

Hay códigos que nacen después de la derrota

       There are codes that are born in the wake of defeat

Llenos de punto y comas. El rumbo que rebota.

       With half-stop periods. The long routes that repeat.

Corchetes o maderos. El detritus que flota.

       Brackets or lumber logs. Sinking detritus fleet.

Patrón de información. Tu cuerpo que se agota.

       Information patterns. Your body in retreat.

Hay islas pixeladas en el largometraje

       Pixelated islands dot blockbuster features.

Multidimensional sin láminas de viaje.

       Multidimensional cries of ghastly creatures.

Las voces digitales trinan en el celaje

       Digital voices trill from the farthest bleachers.

De la isla perdida. Clamor del desencaje.

       A lost island's sermon? Clamor of false preachers.

Hablar curso rimado por la cuaderna vía

    To follow the rhymed course along the fourfold way.

Es orden de galaxias. Luz en apoplejía

    A galactic order. Sun's apoplectic ray

Que deshace mi elipse eclipsando mi día.

    Unravels my ellipse and eclipses my day.

Para tu herida yodo. Miel para tu amnistía.

    Iodine for your wound. Honey for your dismay.

A sílabas contadas se nos suelta un aliento.

    As we count syllables we can hear ourselves breathe.

En la playa fractal del signo un aspaviento.

    Our semiotic beach where signs begin to seethe

Auguros de cadáver. Del revivir del cuento.

    Bathes the fractal corpses that Lethe's cold winds wreathe.

Mental. Monumental. Vacío de momento.

    Mental. Monumental. This void that we unsheathe.

¿Será que tu alarido graniza los pasillos

    Could it be that your cries are hailstones that transfix

Del tedio con iguanas de fragantes colmillos

    The iguanas whose teeth smell like Mayombe sticks

Y orquídeas marchitas? Tu sueño de ladrillos

    And withered blue orchids? Your dream of falling bricks

Dejará los distritos bancarios sin bolsillos.

    Will empty the pockets of the banking districts.

Somos del temporal donde muere la música.

    The storm where music dies gave birth to both of us.

Del cráter perceptual con sus huellas de luz y ca-

    Crater of perception. Its remnants luminous.

lor. Dos constelaciones. Tú y yo. Autobús y ca-

    We're two constellations. Your car next to my bus

rro por la autopista gris, herrumbrada y rústica.

    On the rustic highway. All rust and ferrous pus.

Escrito del esclavo. Con vértigo mi prosa

       To scribble like a slave. My vertiginous prose

Describe un derretir digital de la rosa

       Describes the digital slow dissolve of the rose.

Con grasa simbolista de luna ruborosa

       Oily as a moon blush in late-symbolist throes.

Apostando a morir. Morar en cualquier cosa.

       I bet it all on death. Life takes me where it goes.

Definir el poema que no se codifica

       We define the poem time never codifies

En hilos de sentido y se nos multiplica.

       Into threads of meaning, and so it multiplies.

Su olor de aza(ha)res traspasa la gris mica

       Its random aroma oozes past the gray skies

De la forma perdida o bien se momifica.

       Of a forgotten form, or else it mummifies.

Lenguajes naturales que corren el programa

       Natural languages still program our bodies

Del cuerpo regulado. ¿Por dónde se derrama

       In regulated rhymes born of uncertainties.

Aquel ritmo insular del pitirre sin rama?

       The insular rhythm of sparrows without trees.

¿A qué mar nos condenan? Quemar lo que se ama.

       Waters we must wade in. We burn in our own seas.

Voy por los malecones de tu órbita en ruina.

       I walk along the piers of your orbit in shards

Verde marrón matojo. Abasto de la usina

       Full of greenish-brown shrubs. Stock of solar shipyards.

Solar. Hijo del cielo. Hecho de plasticina

       I'm the son of the sky. Last of the Play-Doh bards.

Tan milenaria y cruel. Mutis que vaticina.

       This cruel and ancient clay. This silence that regards.

La informática lluvia en desierto boreal

    The downpour of data in these boreal sands

Marca coordenadas del cuerpo digital.

    Maps the coordinates of our digital lands.

Conjuga lo imposible. Verbo condicional.

    Impossible verb tense. Our bodies and their brands.

Digital como el dedo con ansias de dedal.

    Digital like fingers who never knew their hands.

Aquestas son las playas que en los videojuegos

    These are the beaches where all the video games

Se pueblan de avatares de olas y hasta luegos

    Are rife with avatars of waves the night misnames.

Acumulando vidas como desasosiegos.

    Accumulating lives like disquieting shames.

Deja que la pantalla te revele sus pliegos.

    Let the screen capture all our ghost mainframes in flames.

La realidad viste esa prenda virtual

    Reality now wears a virtual garment

Del aire que se escapa y el mar de luz marcial.

    In seas of martial light. We lived here when war meant

Cien horas en deshora. Hay un flujo global.

    Our outlaw bodies dead. Until time's disbarment

La pulsión calabozo del palacio animal.

    Set our barracked drives loose like empire's last varmint.

¿Cómo desamarrar el avatar de sesos

    How do we unfasten our avatar of wills

Para que sangre ecos de luz por los pescuezos

    So that it burbles blood in half light through the gills?

En las grandes pantallas? Superávit de huesos.

    Splattering giant screens. Bones crown empire's landfills.

Mil islas reversibles en convertibles pesos.

    Reversible islands on convertible bills.

Luz irrecuperable. Archivo que comprime
> Irreplaceable light. Sound file that compresses

Los instantes e insta la marea a que rime
> Each and every hour marking the tide's stresses.

Roca con *red* y *risco*. Si el ruido no redime
> *Rock* rhymes with *reed* and *ridge*. The sonic abscesses

Basta que nos arrase. Nos bese. Nos lastime.
> In our minds' recesses. Wounds the dark sea blesses.

En la muerte del signo hay códigos que nacen.
> In the death of the sign a new code always thrives.

Saberes que nos sobran. Pulsiones que subyacen.
> All that we know we know. Plus underlying drives.

Dejemos que universos inhóspitos nos tracen.
> Inhospitable worlds contain our afterlives.

Murmullos de criaturas rumiando el almacén.
> Warehoused in warped space-time a new species survives.

[Se escribe con corchetes. Con puntos y sin comas.
> Brackets and periods can measure the biomes.

El mapa cibernético de villorrios y lomas.
> The cybernetic map of hills and spirit homes.

En puras sinestesias. Agrio azul de aromas.
> The synaesthetic sights. Hard acid polychromes.

Los agujeros negros entre los cromosomas.
> The black holes of desire amid the chromosomes.]

(Los paréntesis caen como mustios maderos
> The parentheses fall just like withered lumber

Con incierta frecuencia por los despeñaderos.
> Down stark cliffs now and then like souls into slumber

Tienen la fe absoluta de los unos y ceros
> With absolute faith in gods' binary number

Con que se escribe el eros de días postrimeros.
> And the erotic charge of skies turning umber.)

Hay entre mil patrañas patrón de información.

> Today's tall tales become webs of information

De putrefactas patrias. Nación en pronación.

> In homelands left to rot. Nations in pronation.

Compartimos la diáspora. Solo falta el avión.

> We're one diaspora. Bodies' fraught location.

En tardes de bilharzia y noches de aluvión.

> Reborn after the floods in dark celebration.

Quererte es naufragar en islas pixeladas

> To love you is to drown in pixelated isles

Con ciudades adentro en descuentos de hadas.

> With cities deep inside full of rusted turnstiles

Toditas las palabras serán deletreadas

> Where words go round and round becoming the stockpiles

En las arenas negras del sueño tras las gradas.

> Of black sand in our dream that stretches on for miles.

En tu kaleidoscopio multidimensional.

> Is your kaleidoscope multiverse all-knowing?

¿Ves el antiguo estadio detrás del cafetal

> See the old stadium? Is wild coffee growing

Donde los ciudadanos jugaron al ritual

> Down where the citizens gathered overflowing

De la bala y la vela. Del *buenas* y el *qué tal?*

> For bullet-hole vigils? *Hello. How's it going?*

Los vecinos se hablan en voces digitales

> The neighbors shoot the breeze in digital Creoles.

Como en las bachatas. Clamor de sucursales.

> Bachata choruses fade into night's k-holes.

Hay estacionamientos donde no ponchan vales.

> In trap-beat parking lots a drunken moon patrols.

Palabras pesticidas. Estados vegetales.

> Like pesticides words burn into our rooted souls.

Son transversales siempre las siginificaciones.

    There's a transversal ghost in the self's foundations.

Es un cliché decir que yo soy mis relaciones.

    It's a cliché to say we're webs of relations.

Más bien somos dos ratas trepando zafacones

    I'd say we're two old rats storming trashcan nations

En el Antropoceno sin imaginaciones.

    In the Anthropocene's gnawed imaginations.

Me trepas y te trepo. Me montas y te monto.

    You ride me. I ride you. I climb you. You climb me.

Por el tiempo que dure. Por lo bajo y lo pronto.

    For as long as it lasts with our hands all grimy.

Como feliz bacteria cruzando su Helesponto

    Our hearts somehow intact. Our minds a bit slimy.

De piel a la intemperie con carita de tonto.

    I like you how you are. No need to untie me.

Me montas y te monto. Me trepas y te trepo.

    I climb you. You climb me. You ride me. I ride you.

Me dices al oído lo extraño que te sé(po).

    You say I taste funny. So sweet when I tried you!

Durante la tormenta ya no sé dónde quepo.

    Now the storm swallows us. I feel lost inside you.

Me agarro de la muerte. Tu árbol de quenepo.

    So I hold on to death. It's my turn to guide you.

Terminan los lenguajes. Queda lo que transcribo.

    Languages evanesce. Leaving what I transcribe.

Esa incomodidad de sentirse aún vivo.

    That terrible malaise of feeling half-alive.

Criatura del bosque sin más suelo nativo.

    A forest creature dies. No native soil or tribe.

Máquinas ecocidas compradas sin recibo.

    The ecocide machines compress our diatribe.

Islotes descosidos. Desconocido flujo.

      Unraveled island thoughts flow from an unknown sea.

En la austeridad el orgasmo es un lujo.

      Orgasms are a must under austerity.

La caricia un conjuro y la rima un embrujo.

      Caress means knotted lust. Rhyme is an augury.

Me vengo (de mi suerte). En ti me desdibujo.

      I come (to know myself) in your dark apogee.

CINQUAINS
SIN QUIENES

Anti
            Anti
imperial
            imperial,
leer. Animal canto
            leer. Animal canto
era. De colonial verse
            era. De colonial verse
solo.
            solo.

Primer.
            Primer
Interior
            interior.
fresco. Mar no vital
            Fresco mar. ¿No? Vital
sauce. Taller solar cultivar.
            sauce. Taller solar. Cultivar.
Do come.
            ¿Do come?

Paces.
            Paces.
Habitable
            Habitable
arena. Transversal
            arena. Transversal.
me. He. Tornado. Revolver.
            Me he tornado. Revolver.
Terror.
            Terror.

Rival?

    ¿Rival?

No. Red atlas.

    No. Red. ¿Atlas?

Relieve grave sin? Alas!

    Relieve grave sin alas.

Tender radical. Disparate

    Tender radical. Disparate

seas. Surge!

    seas. ¡Surge!

MOLECULAR MODULAR

lockdown breakdown: DNA sequence of SARS-CoV-2

quebranto de cuarentena: secuencia de ADN del SARS-CoV-2

Ah, you remember when things went viral?
  Acuérdaste de aquel sueño viral?
Can you find lifelines in the death spiral?
  Con vida estás en pírrico espiral?
Goddess, who'll document your retiral?
  Guerreras, ahogarán al admiral?
Time yet for the performative eye roll?
  Tiempo es por fin del guiño neuronal?

Are silences in lines enough spacing?
  Algo en silencio entre líneas pasa?
Can writing be no contact with tracing?
  Cuando se escribe sin contacto es traza?
Graphics matter most when self-erasing?
  Grafía del yo es borradura crasa?
Too soon, on all fours, to start embracing?
  Tarde es para el que, ñangotao, abraza?

Are solemn pages ready for their screen?
  Ante pantallas, página es condena?
Can *quatrains* somehow rhyme with *quarantine*?
  Cuarteto rimará con *cuarentena*?
Gray skies can sometimes signal the unseen?
  Gris cielo al fin o revelación plena?
Trauma was always written in between?
  Trauma es lo que el azar desencadena?

As digital as a corpse orgasm?

        Ay, digital cadáver, y tu orgasmo?

Can poetry be both fold and spasm?

        Cuál poesía: de pliegue o de espasmo?

Gravitas can grow its own sarcasm?

        Gritos de lucha se oyen sin sarcasmo?

Terrors are holes since everyone has 'em?

        Terrenos del terror, dónde me plasmo?

Am I ready for a modular song?

        Atento estoy ante el modular canto?

Can a modular muse ever be wrong?

        Con musa modular cabrá un quebranto?

Grow molecules into a chain that long?

        Grandes moléculas se aferran tanto?

Trembling cells will become a voice how strong?

        Tantas células dan voz al espanto?

ATTAAAGGTT TATACCTTCC . . .

AVE

lockdown song   *canto de cuarentena*
improvising (the Bronx, 05/2020)   *improvisando (el Bronx, 05/2020)*

the birds are back   volvieron las aves   ya tú sabes   comienza otra conversación posible   a new conversation is possible   con el yo interior   with the I within   without what I had   sin lo que tenía   but with what I am   pero con lo que soy   me atrevo   I dare   improvisar   to improvise   some future skies   ciertos cielos futuros

qué más hay   what else is there to do   mientras los pájaros y el tráfico se pelean while the birds and the traffic fight it out   in the shadow of the Bruckner Expressway   bajo la sombra de la autopista Bruckner   en el sur del Bronx   in the South Bronx   donde generaciones de mi gente   where generations of my people   han luchado   have struggled han sobrevivido   have survived   libre albedrío de cantar   the sovereignty of song even amid the distortion   of these technologies   aun en plena distorsión   de tantas tecnologías   otro cuerpo es posible   another body is possible   cuerpos no productivos que no funcionen   unproductive bodies   that don't always work   networked in other ways   desde otro tipo de redes

no te me enredes con lo que digo   don't get tied up with what I'm saying   I mean   tying up is okay if it's consensual   enredarse y atarse está bien si es consensual   pero me interesa   lo natural   but I'm interested   in the natural   flow of the song   el flujo de este canto   en su quebranto   broken but finding its way   pero hallándose sus propios semantemas   its own semantic properties   not all bodies have to be able   no todos los cuerpos tienen que ser capaces   hay otras voces   there are other voices otras maneras de habitar   other ways to inhabit   no need to exhibit   no hace falta exhibir   vivir dentro de sí   y para sí por una vez   to live within oneself   and for oneself for once   enhorabuena   it's about damn time

hubo cruces   hubo diásporas   hubo desplazamientos   hubo muertes   there were crossings   there were diasporas   there were displacements   there were deaths   and there will be more   y más habrá   no obstante aquí estamos   nonetheless here we are cantándoles a los que no están   singing for those who aren't here   pero que están but that are here after all   pero que están aquí después de todo   como el eco del canto de esos pájaros   like the echo of the birds' song   you'll never hear   que nunca oirás porque lo llevas dentro de ti   because you carry it within you   from island to island   de isla en isla   para habitar lo posible   to inhabit the possible

I've been thinking about land lately   llevo pensando en la tierra recientemente   the terrain   el terreno   the territory   el territorio   de la voz   of the voice   donde nos hallamos   where we find ourselves   don't think of this as claustrophobia   no pienses en esto como una encerraera   hay salida   there is a way out   and it's through the voice y es a través de la voz   a través de la voz   trappings of the voice   within and without adentro y afuera   de sí mismo   of oneself   otro ritmo   another rhythm   with em rhythm   with em rhythm   ritmo de uno y con uno   conocerse   to know oneself llamarse   to call oneself   to recall   rememorar   another possible future   otro futuro posible

SOVERANO

Puerto Rico, 07/2019

Ahora te la pasas perdido en el Viejo San Juan, como turista o cachorro en su laberinto.
You're lost all the time in Old San Juan now, like a tourist or a puppy in a maze.

Cuentas los balcones en elegantes ruinas y te preguntas por qué cambiaron los adoquines por estos tan chillones.
You count the elegantly crumbling balconies and wonder when they replaced the cobblestones with these way too shiny ones.

Tocas uno y se siente frío y tieso como risa de político.
You touch one, and it feels as cold and brittle as the smiles of politicians.

Buscas en Google Maps los nombres de los lugares que alguna vez te nombraron.
You check Google Maps to read the place-names that once named you.

Pasas la Plaza de Armas y te acuerdas de la risa oceánica de poetas y pintores compartiendo botellones de vino caliente en vasos plásticos.
You pass Plaza de Armas and remember the oceanic laughter of poets and painters sharing big bottles of lukewarm white wine in plastic cups.

Ya se han ido, muchos muertos, otros a salvo en suburbios o en la diáspora.
They are gone now, mostly dead, some safe in suburbs or in the diaspora.

Y confundes los callejones que eran todo para ti, donde a veces te besaban pero por lo general te quedabas con las ganas, bajo una enorme luna tropical.
And you mix up the alleys that were everything to you, where you were sometimes kissed but mostly hoped you would be, under a huge tropical moon.

Se sienten tan foráneos hoy como los callejones de Wall Street, y con el banquete de los buitres Wall Street nunca está muy lejos.
They feel as foreign as Wall Street alleys now, and with the vultures' ongoing feeding frenzy, Wall Street is never far away.

Y no obstante te hiciste de un alma aquí, una economía afectiva sin desarrolladores.

And yet, you developed a soul here, an affective economy that knows no developers.

Y esa alma ahora les canta a los muertos a quienes todos les debemos.

And that soul now sings through the dead to which we are all indebted.

Muertos de huracán, muertos de austeridad, muertxs de patriarcado, muertos de deudas al blanqueamiento.

Those dead from the hurricane, dead from austerity, dead from patriarchy, dead from whiteness and its debts.

Que vivan los muertos pues todos ellos bailan con nosotros por la plaza y hacia Fortaleza, el palacio de gobierno colonial cuyo nombre es imperio y empuje a la vez.

Praise the dead, for they are all together with us dancing down the plaza and toward Fortaleza, the colonial-era government palace whose name means both *fortress* and *strength*.

No eres tú a la vanguardia: son las mujeres, la juventud, lxs nobinarixs, los de los barrios más pobres.

You are not on the front lines: they are women, they are kids, they are nonbinary, they are from the poorest barrios.

Pero estás con ellos, alentado por su osado gozo, por su certeza que les llegó el momento que es también tu momento, por como se besan hasta el hueso con riguroso embeleso, como querías que te besaran hace tantos años bajo esa misma luna infinita.

Yet you are with them, emboldened by their fearless joy, by their certainty that their time has come and your time as well, by how they kiss each other lazily, with ruthless abandon, as you wish you had been so many years ago under that same boundless moon.

Los tambores convocan al mar de cuerpos hacia Fortaleza hasta que jurarías poder tocarles los chalecos antibalas a los policías y ver tu reflejo en sus cascos.

The drums summon the sea of bodies toward Fortaleza until you swear you could touch the cops' riot gear or see your reflection in their helmets.

Sabes que algunos bailan con ustedes.

You know some of them are dancing with you.

Los encubiertos tirarán basura o fuegos artificiales para justificar balas de goma y gases lacrimógenos que pronto te harán correr al ritmo cadavérico del trap hacia esa pulsión nuestra esmayá y esmameyá más allá del más allá.

Those undercover ones will toss debris or light fireworks to justify the rubber bullets and tear gas you will soon be running from, as reggaetón beats keep the skeletal pulse of our hereafterlives.

Este es nuestro soverano.

This is our sovereign summer.

a missing language **un lenguaje ausente**

CORAL

date cuenta de lo que digo es la voz sin abrigo sin embargo apenas
writing this ink like the inverse of come fulcrum of sweat you end up

puertos ocupados buques sitiados dehiscencia eflorescencia de
with your face in your arms cry if you need to just let those deep breaths

cuerpos sin ciencia cierta la hora muerta la risa la inundación de soles
become one with this hemorrhaging land whose raging hymn will be

que nunca fundaron la nación la consciencia hundida la palabra
born of our hunger with and for each other at the shelled and shellacked

hurtada pero despuntando entre nubes en cromatismos de rabia en
beach there is meager shelter for multitudes of lovers autarkies of capital

atisbos de la luz que nos llama la sílaba que se desparrama por las
the pounding pain of living amid waste and its transfer stations seasons

paredes de la cárcel de un lenguaje por suerte siempre fugitivo en su
of our crossing pulling ourselves over the security fence and onto the

desliz imposible de fijar nos queda nadar hacia el imán del enunciado
beach at the naval base in ruins there is a sunken region where our

la mudez que flota la desnudez que sabe lo que sabe algo así como
bodies change volume visible through what's left of the coral auricular

deliciosa el color de la estrella el calor de otro martes mirándote pintar
song canticle of particles the particleboard of the self as it loses all

un mural de suspiros una instalación de luz amurallada el cemento
particularity becoming particulate protests at the parking lot an

que se sabe montaña o bien arena o bien aire o bien lo húmedo del
enormous bonfire without homes just a pyre of empires an empirical

beso es decir lo cómico de ser sujeto pronominal en calles de fuego
pyrrhic victory vivisection song the threshing machines come for our

encallada hallada la voz coincidencia de piernas fluidos formas
land all we have is our bodies to put in the way on the way toward

escritos de otra tinta rumbo a una libertad coral
a dark ink of fluid forms a choral freedom

missing each other **no tenernos presentes**

ODE TO COFFEE
ODA AL CAFÉ

listening to Juan Luis Guerra
       escuchando a Juan Luis Guerra

from Africa to a Caribbean hill
       de África a las lomas del Caribe
to the smiling ruin of our cities
       a la feliz ruina de ciudades
anoint the neural vessels we refill
       al matorral neural en donde vive
until your acid muse drowns our pities
       tu agria musa que ahoga soledades
return us to our tribe that grew dark beans
       devuélvenos al semillero isleño
cut through the grease of our late-night omelets
       metaboliza la grasa nocturna
and warm this empty diner by the club
       trae tu calor a nuestro desvelo
where luckless lovers stare at tiny screens
       haz que el amante no muera de sueño
and poets brew old socks into psalmlets
       tu borra es poema que embadurna
while dreaming it rains coffee from above.
       y sombría tu alegría de cielo.

we're attuned to the terror **atenernos al espanto**

missing the father and his calls **hace falta el padre y sus llamadas** an incomplete love **un amor incompleto** that sustains us in its own way **que nos sostiene como puede** in the orange hallway **en el pasillo anaranjado** of blazing tropics **y su llamarada de trópicos** when the hurricane goes by **cuando pasa el huracán** a sudden silence **un silencio repentino** that postcards can't fill **que no llenan las postales** we don't remember the rigid body **no recordamos el cuerpo tieso** instead the beaches of our drowned fears **sino las playas de nuestros miedos ahogados** where we were born with you **donde nacimos contigo** the gleam of untold jokes in your eyes **el destello en tus ojos de chistes por decir** now there are lines and blackouts **ahora hay filas y apagones** and media saturation turns hurt into useless rage **y la saturación mediática convierte el dolor en furia inútil** but we see you in the last litoral **pero te vemos en el último litoral** where we are close to you always **donde siempre te tenemos cerca** even as we name your distance **aun cuando nombramos tu distancia** something is blooming in the graveyard of voices **algo florece en el vertedero de voces** it reminds us of what we were that time we walked **nos recuerda lo que fuimos esa vez que caminamos** at your side in the hot night of redwoods **junto a ti coleccionando yagrumos** and it's not the Christian fantasy you hated **y no es la fantasía cristiana que detestabas** to say that we will walk again **decir que caminaremos de nuevo** only this time we'll take photos of the inner precipice **solo que esta vez tomaremos fotos del despeñadero interior** and then we'll laugh like we always did **y luego nos reiremos como de costumbre** and our laughter will become one with the voices of all our dead **y nuestra risa se unirá con las voces de todos nuestros muertos** all of us bathed in light in the unnamed beach **todos bañados de luz en la playa sin nombre** where you taught me how to swim **donde me enseñaste a nadar** and so I swim into the knot of nothingness **y pues nado y la nada es un nudo** that comes undone in our haggard hands **que se deshace en nuestras manos ajadas**

transversal is the light that binds us **transversal es la luz que nos une**

I'm writing you this postcard from the limits of language **te escribo esta postal desde la vera del lenguaje**

the here and there of constellations **el aquí y allá de constelaciones**

this sand we stand on **esta arena que nos sostiene**

puede que te tarde en llegar pero ya la leíste

it may take a while to get there but you already read it

this sand knows **este arenal**

on end **sin final**

it's written in the sand **está escrita en la arena**

this sand of bone **esta arena de huesos**

in memoriam **Thomas L. Noel (1940–2017)**

ABOUT THE AUTHOR

Urayoán Noel is a Puerto Rican poet, performer, critic, translator, and language artist living in the Bronx. He has published seven books of poetry and the study *In Visible Movement: Nuyorican Poetry from the Sixties to Slam* (winner of the LASA Latino Studies Book Prize and an MLA Honorable Mention), and he has been a finalist for the National Translation Award and the Best Translated Book Award for his solo and group translations of Latin American poetry. His international performances include Poesiefestival Berlin, Barcelona Poesia, and the Toronto Biennial of Art, and his work has been selected for exhibition at the Museum of the City of New York, the Museo de Arte de Puerto Rico, and Taller Boricua. Noel is currently an associate professor of English and Spanish and Portuguese at New York University, a Schomburg Center Scholar-in-Residence, and a member of the CantoMundo steering committee.